Exit First

Exit First

How to Make Extraordinary
Profits from
Ordinary Auctions

by Rick Rickert

On the Inside Press
Beverly Hills, CA

Exit First: How to Make Extraordinary Profits from Ordinary Auctions

info@infoclosure.com
www.infoclosure.com

Published by On the Inside Press
Beverly Hills, CA 90210
www.OntheInsidePress.com

Library of Congress Control Number 2015901775
ISBN 978-1-942707-04-2

Cover design by Carli Smith and David T. Fagan. Edited by Michael McCall

This publication is designed to provide authoritative information with regard to the subject matter covered. It is sold with the understanding that neither the author nor the publisher is engaged in rendering legal, accounting or other professional service. If legal advice or other expert assistance is required, the services of a competent professional person should be sought.

Acknowledgements

I would like to take a moment and thank the following people who without their inspiration and help this book would not have come about.

To my parents; Joe and Pat Rickert, thank you for always being the open and loving people you are. To my Dad who never backed down from a repair job on a house. You were my original inspiration to get into real estate investing.

To my children and grandchildren; Nikki, Joe, AJ, Jada, and Annalisse. You are the most beautiful souls I have ever met. Thank you for being such a huge part of my life.

To the many people who assisted in putting this book together; David Fagan, thank you for the great ideas including the cover and title. Jill Fagan, thank you for your expertise in publishing. To all those on my staff for your contribution: Michael McCall, Chris Lembke, Alyssa Geyer, David Simon, Kevan Neyestani, Elliott Utley, Joe Rickert and Nikki Wooldridge.

Table of Contents

Foreword

This book was written specifically for two groups of people – those involved in real estate investing and those thinking about becoming involved. Although group one is a step ahead of group two in the process, both stand to learn a great deal from reading this book. The fact that you have this volume in your hands (or perhaps on your screen), means you definitely belong to one of these groups. Wherever you are in your investing career, this book will explore a method of real estate acquisition which has been around for a long, long time, but one which few have taken advantage of for various reasons.

In the early 1600's, the famous Italian physicist, astronomer and engineer, Galileo, was sent to prison for arguing that the earth was not flat, but round. Galileo was one of several enlightened individuals of his time who most certainly thought outside the box, who had a store of knowledge that most of his peers did not have, and was not afraid to embrace that knowledge. Why was most of the world so threatened by Galileo's theories? The answer is timeless and simple. The world did not understand what he was talking about, was very complacent in a different way of thinking, and was very openly afraid of what they did not comprehend. What the world held as sacred truth for centuries was being threatened by new knowledge.

So, you're asking yourself what a round earth has to do with trustee sales and enjoying extraordinary profits! Great question. There's a particular phrase that is repeated often in this book and that is, "You don't know what you don't know". People in Galileo's era didn't know what they didn't know. I don't mean to infer that a controversial investment strategy in our time is as profound as Galileo and a round earth, but I venture to guess you're getting the idea. Many investors have heard about public real estate auctions and have avoided them because of fear, what others have said, something they've read, oh, and did I mention fear? Fear comes from the fact that this method of acquisition is different from the way you "think" you know it; it ventures out and away from the standard way we've been exchanging real estate for decades. I've heard many investors run screaming from the idea of public

auction saying that the risks are too great. When I finally catch up with them and ask what they think these horrible risks are, they really don't know – and what they think they know isn't reality.

That's why this book was written. It's going to methodically take you through the process of acquiring real estate using this relatively easy method. Please note that the terms "public auction" and "trustee sale" are used interchangeably throughout the coming chapters. While all public auctions are not necessarily trustee sales, and while the focus is on the latter, the principles you're going to learn are applicable to both. The book takes you through all the "true" risks, debunks those that just aren't real, and lays out exactly what to watch for and be careful of. More importantly, the author pays special attention to what *not* to do in order to realize extraordinary gains from ordinary auctions.

Among others, this book examines the most basic areas of this method of property acquisition such as:

- ✓ Exit Strategies – Perhaps the most important of all. The exit strategy really determines how much your investment will yield and how long it will take.

- ✓ Starting Out – Depending on whether you're in group one or two, the fundamental pieces of the puzzle that must be present and integrate properly before you begin in order to ensure success.

- ✓ Knowledge – This is your source of power. Finding the information you need before you spend precious dollars, parsing and making sense of the data.

- ✓ Learning – Taking long enough to become familiar with the process before diving in.

- ✓ Who's Who? – Knowing the various players in the game. Figuring out whether you're going to become the quarterback or the linebacker.

- ✓ Risks – Discovering what they really are and how to mitigate them properly, using specific schedules of due diligence before and after a purchase, so that they become benefits.

- ✓ Psychology – This should perhaps be at the top of the list. Learn the games people play at an auction, how to become acutely aware of their subtleties, and use them to your advantage without becoming mired in them.

As a business person and artist, I've always tried to surround myself with people who know more than I do and are better at certain skills than I am. This way I've got something to work toward and will learn on the way. For the last several years, I've had the pleasure to work with and observe the author of this book, Rick Rickert. Rick is an absolute expert at what he does, and like any good artist, is passionate about it. You'll see as you read

EXTRAORDINARY

through this book that he has achieved extraordinary success using the methods and processes he's laid out for you. Enjoy this journey through Rick's 16 plus years of investing experience, while you learn from his mistakes and his triumphs. Most of us don't get a chance to avoid blunders when we head into something new. This book gives you that advantage.

When Galileo began to proclaim that the earth was round, he took a profound and bold step. However, when he did so, it was not without knowledge and confidence to back up his claim. (Ok, he did end up behind bars, but thank goodness the world has progressed a little since then!) I want to congratulate you for beginning this book – you've taken a bold step.

You've decided to put aside your fears and doubts and gain a bit of real knowledge. You've decided you need to find out what the real story is. That's the first key to success. You're well on your way to leaving ordinary behind. You're on the first leg of your journey to the extraordinary.

Michael McCall
Designated Broker, Look Inside Realty

Chapter 1

Exit Strategies

"Begin with the end in mind."

Peter Drucker

While there are three exit strategies that will be outlined in this chapter, one in particular has been my primary focus since the beginning. I started out in the business as a "fix-and-flip" guy. I chose that direction because it was my desire to receive relatively quick cash profits from my investments. Knowing I wanted to pull

Gain the knowledge you need before acting!

fast cash out of deals meant the fix-and-flip strategy was the obvious choice. It wasn't until years later that I realized just how important establishing an exit strategy was. For several years already, I had been teaching the foreclosure auction approach to investors. It wasn't until an attendee came to me after a particular class, looked me straight in the eye and asked, "Rick, what IS the first step?" That question was so profound, I rewrote all my material after that and coined the phrase "Exit First". It was painfully obvious, but I hadn't considered that some people would consider an acquisition method without knowing or having a clearly defined exit strategy. From that point forward, I spent a great deal of time outlining various exit strategies and helping investors accurately evaluate their real estate investment programs, thereby making property selection so much more straightforward. There is real estate that is very appropriate for quick liquidation and fast cash (fix-and-flip) as well as other choices more appropriate for long term buy-and-hold (rental). Understanding this is critical to making the best intelligent exit strategy choices.

There is an important distinction that needs to be examined and it boils down to one question every investor should ask: "What is the result I want from purchasing this property?" The answers are relatively easy: "I want quick profit from the flip, tax benefits and appreciation profit from the hold, or 'really fast cash' (smaller amount) from wholesaling."

I said earlier that fix-and-flip was my preferred investment strategy from the beginning. Let me be crystal clear. It was also my exit strategy while investing full time in real estate. Two years prior to leaving

corporate America, I got a call from my CPA Mike. I talked to Mike about twice a year, in April and in October. Our October conversation is usually a strategy session looking at both short term and long term plans. One year he said there was only so much he could do to reduce my tax base and his suggestion was to offset my income with rental properties. This would provide me with benefits such as deductions and write-offs in the short term, cash flow in the interim period, and wealth building appreciation in the long term. He gave me new strategies to offset income with write-offs that had a long term upside. Most new investors don't understand these concepts regarding rental real estate investment. Some of them are not and never will be short term plays. There is a lot of cash in the short term coming out of pocket and many think it isn't supposed to work that way. More about that later.

There are three basic exit strategies in real estate investing, however one of them isn't exclusively an exit, but also a hold strategy. Now stop for a second and get your mind around this. Conceptually, it is still an exit strategy, as there will come a time, perhaps many years from now, when you will no longer own the property!

I'm devoting an entire chapter on exit strategies because they are so important to understand. Exit strategies will often determine your purchase strategy as you will see coming up. So let's get right into the three strategies of the serious real estate investor.

Fix-and-Flip

This is the most popular of all the strategies and is the favored approach for as much as 80% of the investors I have worked with, and also my personal strategy for the majority of properties I have purchased at foreclosure auctions.

This one is really simple. Buy at the lowest possible under market price, do some minimal repairing and cosmetic upgrades, and then sell immediately at market price. Put your profit in the bank and repeat!

If it were really this easy...

Buying at public auction is significantly different from traditional real estate. One of the major challenges that goes with the territory is that you don't get the opportunity to inspect the property and perform typical due diligence prior to bidding. Continue reading and do not fear! In a later chapter on driving properties, I go into greater detail about getting the edge on repair analysis. This one challenge will keep novice investors away from the auction space and I have no issue with

this. This is one of two areas where investors can make costly mistakes. Now let's be clear— I am not trying to scare you out of this space. In fact, this book is dedicated to providing you with the knowledge and tools to apply these principles in any market and profit successfully from what learn. I have successfully bid on and purchased many homes I had never seen the inside of. Yes, it is risky, but it is also part of the fun of buying at auction.

The strategy may be simple, but the realities may be very different.

Occasionally, repairs needed will be more expensive than planned.

There may be an unexpected and costly repair necessary that you won't discover until after you have made the purchase.

It may take much longer to sell than anticipated forcing you to pay the holding costs for longer than expected.

Market downturns can force you to sell for a lower price than originally planned.

The smart and successful real estate investor learns how to mitigate these risks, and the processes for doing so. Every investor needs to understand and accept the fact that no

The picture shown is the first house I purchased at auction in 1998. When I won the bid I had mixed emotions; total excitement and on the other hand complete nervousness as to what was behind the locked door all this while maintaining my poker face.

matter which strategy they use; no matter how experienced they become; no matter how many properties they purchase – they will eventually end up with a property that makes no profit or may even result in a loss.

In my investment career, I have purchased approximately 200 properties implementing the fix-and-flip strategy and have broken even on four, and lost a little on two. Not a bad average, considering I made considerable profit on the majority of those 200 deals. However, I was lucky enough not to acquire the losses early in my career. On all six of my buys that were not profitable, there were expensive repairs that were not apparent when I placed my bids.

In addition to unexpected repairs, market conditions can adversely affect your transaction. For example, no matter what level of accurate care you use in analyzing  comparable properties to establish your selling price, appraisers typically have the final say and it may not be what you expected. Personally, I prefer the $100,000 to $250,000 price range for selling homes. There are a variety of reasons for this, but suffice it to say that this range makes them ultimately eligible for a FHA loan. FHA's were initially created to help those who could not qualify for anything conventional. As the years have progressed, more and more individuals cannot obtain a typical conventional loan, making the FHA option the popular sub-prime solution in the market today. Result: The number of FHA borrowers out there has significantly increased your buyer pool.

Again, two important components can have adverse effects on your deals. Unknown repairs and market conditions. The best way to hedge against these risks is to surround yourself with qualified professionals as you get ramped up. Experience will serve you well in the long term.

In most instances, there are certain repairs that cannot be deferred. For example, a slab leak, where a water pipe under the foundation is broken or leaking, must be repaired. Any structural problem with weight bearing consequences must be addressed. Plumbing and electrical problems must be fixed. These are just a few examples.

Depending on local laws, you may be required to use licensed contractors and secure building permits, pay fees, etc. It is important to know the laws in your state regarding licensed work requirement and permits. You don't want to get mired in city or county regulation disputes. Typically, a fix-and-flip requiring minor work won't be a problem, but I have had projects that were in need of a lot of repair and I was forced to get proper permits as well as have inspections performed.

A short time ago, I bought every multi-family "plex" I could get my hands on. In one particular case, I acquired a six-plex comprised of two separate triplexes on the same parcel. The property had been vacant for a long while and had also been vandalized prior to auction. I knew it was in rough shape but also knew that as long as it could be acquired for a low enough price, the deal would make sense. I purchased it for $58,000. Less than $10,000 per door makes sense as far as I'm concerned anytime. In addition to typical remodeling, paint and carpet, etc., there were two costly repairs. I found it necessary to re-wire the property, including electrical panels, and also to re-plumb the property. Here were two examples of what I referred to earlier as repairs that could not be deferred. I recently sold the property and maximized my profit by splitting the property with the county assessor and sold the two triplexes individually instead of one combined parcel. Typically, a multi-family property comprised of four units or more is considered commercial and thus requires commercial financing. By splitting the parcel, I took complex financing out of the equation and increased my overall profit by 15%!

Thankfully, these are the exceptions and not the rule. The majority of homes I purchased needed only paint, new carpet, and some landscaping improvements and sold quickly at their full market value.

The bottom line is that you must understand the risks before diving in! That's why they call it investing.

I am often asked why I buy at the foreclosure auction almost exclusively. It's simple. The auction is the ONLY place I know of where properties can be acquired by the individual investor at prices significantly below actual market value! In most cases these properties are not on an MLS (Multiple Listing Service). I'm a licensed real estate broker and I can tell you that everything listed with the MLS is at or very near market value. I am not saying the MLS is useless, quite the opposite. It is a critical tool for investors. It's just that I can consistently find below market deals every day and acquire them within days – not weeks or months. I do not rule out the MLS as an inventory source and in fact purchase from there occasionally, but those account for less than three percent of what I have done with flips.

In order to make money on fix-and-flip investing, there needs to be a sufficient spread between the buying price – that is the price you pay to acquire the property– and the actual market value of like properties in that area. If that's not the case, you will lose dearly earned money! An investor must also consider properties whose eventual selling prices (the fair market value), fall into a range that most people can afford.

The Phoenix market, in which I have the most experience, the eventual target selling price is approximately $180,000 or less in the metropolitan area. A home in good condition, on the market in that price range will be a fairly easy and quick sell. Remember, each month a property sits on the market is another month you are stuck with the holding costs.

So, if there is a property coming up for sale at auction in a neighborhood in which the average market value is approximately $180,000, to what level can you raise your maximum bid and still have the necessary spread? Well, there are many variables involved, but if you can acquire that property for $140,000 or so, there is a distinct possibility you will make a nice profit. Now that's just a profile; you must do your own due diligence, which we will address later in this book.

There are areas in the Phoenix, Arizona market where foreclosures with a wide spread can be found, but where actual market prices, when repaired and "sell ready", will be over $300,000 and beyond. As acquisition prices go upward over the average home price in the area, your holding costs are going to be proportionately greater as the pool of buyers who can actually qualify to buy such a home diminishes. How long will they remain on the market before they're sold? No one knows, but the risk can be significantly reduced by working within these price range areas and with a Realtor® who specializes in that area.

One can get lucky from time to time and find someone who is looking for exactly what you have and can afford it. Luck, however, does not factor into any of my investment strategies, nor should it in yours! As a fix-and-flipper, I want to be in and out in 90 days.

As any Realtor® can tell you, as the selling price goes up, the longer it takes to sell. If you want to fix-and-flip, stay near the average price for a home in that area and avoid long selling cycles.

I want to leave you with my fix-and-flip key to success. In 2004 I got my home inspector license. I had plans to build a large home inspection company, which obviously never happened and is a topic for another book entitled "All the

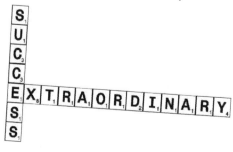

Businesses I Have Thought of Starting". The point is, every time I sold a property, the buyer brought in a home inspector and I ended up with a massive list of items to correct. Having my inspector's license helped me to identify the items that were going to be called out and potentially ruin my deal. The reality is the buyer and their agent typically show up at the inspection and inspectors have a hard time curbing both verbal and non-verbal (body language) disappointment about all the problems found in the home. Inspectors are often to blame for scaring off buyers before the needed repairs are negotiated.

All right, here's the key to success in this: I engage a home inspector for all my fix-and-flip deals prior to starting any remodeling. The cost of the inspection is minimal compared to the cost of a buyer walking away from my house. I have it inspected and consequently hand the report to my crew who then complete everything on the list as well as the cosmetic items like paint and carpet. Again, I do this up front, well before I even try to sell the property.

Now, when the buyer's inspector talks about the property, they have probably found very little wrong and their body language and conversations are substantially different which create a high degree of buyer confidence and keeps them in play.

Smart investors will pick up on this immediately and implement this crucial step in the process. The rest will try to save the inspection fees and lose 10 to 20 times that amount in carrying costs – because buyers keep walking from the deal.

Buy and Hold

Before I get into the detail of this section, I want to give you some idea of what to expect. Most investors believe that keeping properties and collecting rents is easy. I can't tell you how many times I run into investors desperate to unload a property they have owned for a year or less. That makes no sense to me and after they tell me their reasons for selling, typically it makes even less sense. The primary reason to take on hold properties or rental properties, is long term wealth building. There's a reason they're called "income producing" properties, and along with that kind of investment comes great tax write offs and other tax related benefits. Long term! It is not uncommon to operate at a very low cap rate the first year or two while you are working through repairs and tenant issues. Cash flow is important, but secondary to the appreciation of the asset over the longer term. If cash flow is the only thing you, as the investor is looking for, I can direct you to several safe alternative investments that don't have all the day to day hassles that rental properties can have. I often recommend that investors buy notes and be a "note holder". Notes are a great way to profit from real estate without buying it, selling it or managing it. With that said, fortunes are made through the buy-and-hold strategy. Buying at auction is the best starting point, as you have built in equity from the start – at acquisition time – making your cap rate that much higher.

With a buy-and-hold strategy, you make the initial repairs, find a tenant, and sell at a later date when market conditions are more favorable. This provides you with monthly income and the probability of a much higher resale price down the road. And that's the risk!

No one has a crystal ball, and if you ask 10 real estate 'experts' what the market will be like in two or five years from now, you will get 10 different opinions. Generally speaking however, over time real estate appreciates; this is borne out by so much historical data that it's practically indisputable. But in the march up, there have been periods when prices slid backward. Consider the housing bust of 2007!

However, as fast as home prices fell during the crash, they are now slowly but surely moving upward. Areas that were affected most by the housing bubble, like Phoenix and Las Vegas, also have had the biggest gains following the market crash.

Something else to consider with the buy-and-hold strategy is that you become a landlord, with all the issues that come with this esteemed status. Tenants who don't pay or are habitually late with their rent, frantic calls at 2 am about how they are locked out, the toilet is overflowing, the air conditioning isn't working, and the list goes on.

For some, these problematic situations are no deal killer. Certain individuals can deal with these issues without losing their cool. For others, it's a non- stop nightmare that seems to never end.

If you are going to employ the buy and hold strategy, I urge you to talk to other landlords first. This method is a proven and effective one – simply go in with eyes wide open. I own a number of rental properties and they're a mixed bag. Some tenants I don't hear a peep from and they pay their rent on time month after month. Some have been more difficult!

If you acquire a number of properties, you may want to look into professional management. Yes, they take a share of the gross rents, but they effectively remove 90% of the headaches. They screen prospective tenants, they take the 2 am emergency calls, and they collect the rents and pay you as well as taking care of those tenants who don't pay or are late. This is the route I have taken with my rental properties and I highly recommend it.

Now for the good news! You get a steady, reliable income every month, which goes up as the rents go up. You get value appreciation of the property over time. And you get favorable tax treatment, thanks to the miracle of depreciation, which shields a portion of your rental income from Uncle Sam. Make sure you consult your tax professional, as this can be very technical. You don't want to have unnecessary problems with the tax boys!

Lastly, there is an IRS protection plan in place for long time owners to dispose of fully depreciated property without having to pay capital gains taxes. It's a provision in the tax code called a 1031 exchange that lets you sell at a profit without any taxes due, as long as you don't take constructive control of the proceeds, and reinvest it in a 'like' property within a specified period of time, thus escaping taxes due on the capital gain. Again, it is important that you talk to your CPA or tax advisor about this, as the rules are set out in the IRS code and must be followed to the letter.

So buy-and-hold is a very viable strategy as long as you can handle the landlord aspect and are knowledgeable about the special tax advantages of owning rental property.

With either of these strategies, there is often another factor to deal with, the contractor. My advice: Unless you are a contractor yourself with considerable experience in remodeling homes, or have a friend in the industry, tread very carefully. Dealing with contractors can be one of the most frustrating experiences you will ever have. As with any service you are forced to hire, be familiar with as many possible. Interview as many companies as you can; discover their work ethic, find out which of them will give you the best discounts, etc. More importantly, get referrals from others. Investigate their completion time history. Do they finish a job when they say they will? I've said this several times already, but time delays eat into your profits.

- *Purchase price $21,200*
- *4-plex, 50% occupied*
- *Sold for $75,000*

Albert Einstein said, "All time is relative", and contractors have taken this concept to the extreme. "In a few hours" could mean next week, 'tomorrow' might mean some other tomorrow than the day after today. It can be difficult to plan the job properly if both you and the contractor are working on different timelines. If the electricians can't do their job, for example, before the cabinet guys can come in, and the cabinets are late, this can hold up every other area of the job.

Contractors are not bad guys, but yours is not the only job they have going at any one time. They constantly pull workers from one job to send to another because another client is yelling louder than you! This constant juggling of their employees means that four are there one day, the next only one shows up! Your urgency is not their urgency. So consider that more time might be needed than you believe is necessary to complete the remodel.

Notwithstanding the possible obstacles, lots of people are making lots of money at it. At the risk of being repetitive, the key to your success is being able to obtain the property at a price significantly under market value,  and this is most often the case with distressed properties. One of my regular clients follows this strategy. He is a retired general contractor with extensive knowledge and insider contacts in every industry. For him, it works very well, but again, I can't advise people without that kind of background to attempt this.

Let me summarize this before we go on. Your exit strategy ultimately depends on what you want as an investor. If you want to generate quick profits, fix-and-flip. If you want to build long term wealth, consider building a portfolio of rental properties using a buy-and-hold strategy. Acquiring properties through auction supports all of these strategies beautifully.

Wholesaling

When I started buying at public auction, the majority of my competition was wholesalers. Their basic model was to buy a property at auction, mark the price up and immediately sell it. The keys to effective wholesaling are:

- Source of inventory
- Hard money or line of credit
- Immediately accessible pool of buyers

You can create a successful business by serving investor clients when you have all three components in alignment. One of the big mistakes new wholesalers make is to not have their buyers lined up before purchasing. Even worse is to buy something your buyers won't want.

I created what I call a modified wholesale platform that has served me well since 2000 and still does today. Through one of my companies, INFOclosure.com, we provide investors access to the auction space who agree to compensate us for a successful bid at auction. They get access to the list of upcoming auction properties. They do their own analysis from information I provide as well as utilizing their own evaluation methods. We provide pre-auction due diligence, property videos, lien positions, and delinquent tax information.

To break down the keys to success in wholesaling, a first consideration is the inventory source. I have found that the auction space allows for a consistent flow of properties at the lowest price point in the market. In addition to that, you are buying within a structure that allows for the fastest acquisition time in the market. All wholesalers should be utilizing the auction space for their buys.

Keep in mind, investors only want properties with a sufficient margin and the sooner they get them the better.

The second key to success is access to hard money or a line of credit. Unless you have unlimited amounts of cash in the bank, you will need to leverage the purchase. Your capital structure should ideally contain no points and hopefully carry a reasonable interest rate. Keep in mind, when wholesaling, a high interest rate won't be very relevant, but points will. Later in the book we'll talk in much more detail about hard money and leveraging the purchase.

And last, but certainly not least, is having ready buyers. Never buy a property to wholesale on speculation. You have to have a buyer you know with relative certainty will take the property within 48 hours. If you hold a property longer than that amount of time, you're out of alignment with what I call good wholesaling. Early on, I observed the practices of wholesalers I competed against and decided I didn't want to take on the risks they were shouldering. As I mentioned earlier, I created a modified process for wholesaling and it has served me

well and virtually eliminated my risk of holding properties. One last note on wholesaling: Holding title in your name prior to conveyance to your wholesale buyer is most often a mistake. This can cause "chain of title" issues. Most properties today are ultimately bought with FHA financing and FHA does not like to see "flipping" on the title report during their loan underwriting. When we buy at auction for an investor client, the property is titled directly to the investor, not to us, which eliminates title snags when they ultimately sell to the party planning on living in the property.

Within these parameters, you need to be a real bargain hunter. In wholesaling, properties must be bought at rock bottom prices and sold as soon as possible to rehabbers, those who implement major rebuilding on their acquisitions and then sell for larger profits. Many investors like to buy distressed properties because they are in various stages of disrepair. When such properties are wholesaled, the typical profit is only around $5000. Be that as it may, it's a really quick $5000 and if you can transact enough of these, there's an appreciable amount of profit waiting for you.

Lease Purchase

The lease purchase strategy is rarely used by the smaller investor. While I personally do not use it often, I have had great success with it in the past. It is a hybrid between "fix-and-flip" and "buy-and-hold". Purchasing at public auction is, as always, a great source for properties to utilize in this arena.

The fundamental premise is to buy a property, improve it to move in ready condition and make it attractive enough for a quality tenant.

This is a good time to go off-topic for a moment and make an important distinction regarding two different "ready" home conditions. When doing any kind of rehab to a property (assuming you're not going to live in it yourself), you're either going to bring the property to a "rent ready" condition or a "sell ready" condition. Exact definitions and descriptions of those are subjective and will vary from house to house and person to person, but suffice it to say you're not going to do as much to a home in getting it ready to rent as you might when preparing the same property to sell.

Back to the lease-purchase option. The tenant you're looking for here is not your average tenant. This party is most often a serious buyer, but without the ability at the time to secure the loan needed. This party is interested in leasing the home they fall in love with for a year or two and when all their ducks are finally in a row, purchase said home. This party is going to be the home owner at a future date – your buyer.

Your financial objective is to maximize your return by allowing market appreciation to work in your favor over the next one to two years. The structure is relatively simple. You're going to use two documents for the exit. First is the purchase contract and second is the lease agreement. Consult an experienced attorney or real estate professional when doing this the first time. The devil is truly in the details. Here are a few things to consider. When taking a deposit, make sure it is earnest money for the purchase and not a lease deposit. You will use specific language (that I share later in this chapter) to protect your investment. Also, when setting the future sale price, you have two things to consider. List it as "market value" to be determined at the average of two appraisals 30 days

prior to closing on the purchase, or pick a price. If you pick a price (which is what I typically do) you can inadvertently leave money on the table. The price you pick can be today's value or today's value plus a percentage per year appreciation. Choosing market price at the time of closing also has a down side as it will work against you if the market drops and can force a loss unless you choose to breach the contract.

There are several moving parts to this strategy, so I will list them and then go deeper into each one.

- Purchase a property below market value
- Improve the house to move in ready condition
- Find a viable tenant/buyer
- Use the proper documents
- Understand the Market

In order for this strategy to be successful, you need to know with some level of certainty that the market will go up. Work with two or more real estate professionals to determine the best area for this exit strategy. You are looking for a price point that works for the majority of the market, so stay in the range of the average priced home or slightly above. You want 80% of the market to be able to afford your house. The most recent one I did dropped right into the range I was looking for. I purchased it at $170,000 with the intent to sell it at $245,000 two years later. I purchased the home in 2011 and it would not appraise at that time for $245,000. The idea was to get the appreciation over a one to two year period and maximize the profit. This is a bit of a "futures" game to truly maximize the profit. Let me explain by giving more details. The day I purchased the property, I knew it would not appraise for more than $225,000. I decided this would be a great property for lease-purchase because that particular area was popular and I was confident the area would appreciate over the next two years. The question is, of course, how much would it appreciate? No one ever knows the exact answer to that.

Purchasing a property below market

Without question, the purchase of the house came through public auction, and again, that is the focal point of this book. Had I purchased the house for less than what I did, I would have flipped it for a quick profit. I won't elaborate further on the buy at auction because the remaining chapters of this book take care of that for us.

Improving the house to "move in ready" condition

As I mentioned a short time ago, preparing a house for fix-and-flip ("sell ready") is fundamentally different than making a property "rent ready" and going into a lease purchase strategy falls somewhere in between. I don't do every repair I normally would with a lease purchase as I do with a fix-and-flip, but pretty close. The house will get more cosmetic upgrades as opposed to the bigger ticket items that may be close to, but not at the end of their functional life. Granite counter tops, fresh interior paint, new carpet, and professional cleaning are items I typically take care of to get the best possible tenant/buyer into the house.

Find a viable Tenant/Buyer

There are a lot of reasons for someone to want to do a lease purchase transaction. Again, the biggest benefit for the tenant/buyer is getting into a property they can't qualify for today. This strategy allows people access knowing they need to qualify on or before the end of the lease period. I typically ask for $5,000 or $10,000 as down payment for the purchase and only refundable if the house does not appraise. Below is common language I use on the counter offer of the purchase contract.

"Buyer agrees that the earnest deposit is a deposit for the purchase of the property."

"Buyer agrees that no portion of the monthly lease payment goes towards the purchase of the property."

"Buyer agrees that the earnest deposit is only refundable if the property does not appraise."

"Buyer agrees that the earnest deposit is non-refundable in the event buyer fails to qualify for a loan to purchase."

Refer to your broker or attorney before adding the suggested language. While these statements on contracts have served me well in Arizona, they have not been proven in other states.

Use the appropriate documents

In every state, a valid real estate contract must be in writing and executed by both parties. My recommendation is always use the same contracts as

the real estate community uses. The primary reason is that the language has already been proven in court and supported by your state's department of real estate.

- *Purchase price $1,650,000*
- *96 unit multi-family complex "C"*
- *Sold (8 months later) $2,200,000*

While you can write a contract on a napkin and it will be valid, I do not recommend it. Stick with what has been proven over time – it's worth it. Most real estate professionals will provide you with a complimentary copy of any contract. Working through an attorney is also a good idea when starting out. There's no reason to learn by making mistakes others have already made when there are professionals standing by ready to give assistance. I will say it again... one or two hours of an attorneys' time is priceless. I know what you're thinking and I've been there too. "I am just starting out, I don't want to, or think I can't afford to use an attorney". In most cases you can't afford not to.

> **Important Concepts**
>
> 1. Choose an exit strategy prior to looking at properties.
> 2. Become a master at that strategy to maximize profits.
> 3. Consider a joint venture or partnership while you are working on mastery.

Chapter 2

Fundamentals and Getting Started

"Success is neither magical nor mysterious. Success is the natural consequence of consistently applying the basic fundamentals."

Jim Rohn, American speaker and author

In any endeavor, be it business, athletic, or any other you can name, a basic understanding of the fundamentals is crucial to success. Venturing into the foreclosure auction space is no different. I have seen many investors get into it without a basic understanding of the rules of the game and get badly burned.

There will always be risk, but it can be hugely minimized.

Real estate investing has its own set of rules. There are procedural rules that are often governed by law, and other rules of investing that apply. Investing in real estate involves risk, and the rules that I will talk about in this chapter have a lot to do with *minimizing* that risk. You cannot remove risk entirely, but you can follow rules that stack the deck in your favor.

I highly recommend talking to two different professionals when getting started. First, a CPA. I always want the highest and best leverage regarding taxes when setting up. Second is a seasoned real estate attorney. It is critical to have proper structure (outside of tax issues) to protect your assets when investing. I have been asked on many occasions, "Rick, what should I do? Set up an LLC for each property I buy?" The answer will always come back to the professionals you work with and their estimation of the best choices for you based on your financial situation. Personally, I have about a dozen LLCs. When it comes to investing, I do all my flips in one, all my buy-and-holds in another, and typically start a new one when entering into a joint venture or partnership.

Arizona is one of the easiest and most cost effective states in which to open an LLC. It takes less than an hour and under $100 to get it going. Not every state makes it so easy, so seeking professional help is always wise. I'm a big advocate of using professional services to do the things I'm not qualified to do! Also, if investing becomes a full time effort, then you will have to rely on other people to do certain things for you, or you will find yourself working 25 hours a day.

The primary reason for an LLC structure is to separate various activities and provide you with protection for your personal assets. The forming of an LLC or corporation shields your personal assets from creditors if something goes wrong in your investing activities. Keep in mind, however, that nothing protects you from fraud or misrepresentation.

In every state I am aware of, LLC's are usually created and filed with the Secretary of State's office. Then you can obtain a business license. In some states, you actually go to the state offices, file the documents personally and receive your business license in the mail within a few days. In others, there are online resources that can make your appearance in person unnecessary.

With a business license in hand, you can open a business checking account. Banks will typically not allow you to open a business account without showing them a business license. You'll also need a federal tax ID number which is obtained in minutes at www.irs.com. It is important to use your new business account when making investment related purchases – don't comingle your personal funds with your investment dollars! Now, after you have taken care of these two things, you are ready to start learning about the foreclosure auction.

What Happens At The Foreclosure Auction?

A lot of what we are going to learn comes from my personal experience in Arizona, Nevada, California, and Florida. Though similar to what happens in counties all over the US, there are also basic differences from state to state. However, the underlying principle is the same.

There are two types of foreclosure processes in the United States, judicial and non-judicial. Non-judicial states are typically those in the western part of the country. Eastern states primarily implement a judicial process, but it is important to know that non-judicial foreclosure states may use judicial proceedings as well. The end result may be similar, but the process is not.

In the judicial process, the mortgage is the security instrument for the loan. When the buyer is in default, he/she is served with a *Notice of Default*. If the default is not remedied in the time period provided, the case will most often go to court and the buyer is served with a *Notice of Sheriff's Sale*, which informs them of the date on which the property will be sold at a Sherriff's Sale. On the date of the auction, the winning bidder is assigned a Sheriff's Deed to the property.

In a non-judicial process, a Deed of Trust is the security instrument for the loan. When a buyer defaults, he/she is served with a similar *Notice of Default*, followed by a *Notice of Trustee Sale*. The winning bidder at the trustee sale is given a Trustee's Deed to the property.

Keep in mind, if a property is going to auction today, the process it went through to get there is not nearly as important to me as pre-auction due diligence as well as post auction issues. Let me explain. Whether I buy a property in Florida under their judicial system or buy one in Arizona's non-judicial system, I am more concerned with other issues. Those most concerning me prior to the sale are: lien position, county taxes in arrears, city assessments that survive the sale, HOA liens, mechanics liens, etc.

Each state has its own laws governing the foreclosure process. Some of those laws state very clearly which liens survive the foreclosure sale and those that do not. In states that use vague and ambiguous language, it would be best to consult a real estate attorney and talk to the title company you will be using. In Chapter 8 we go more deeply into pre-sale due diligence, but understand that a sizable lien that legally stays with the property is something preferably discovered before you lay out your cash!

Often, an opening bid at auction is well below the actual market value of comparable homes in that area. Here again is the primary reason investors bid on and buy properties at auction. They want to acquire property below market value! This is especially true of 'fix-and-flip' investors, who are the majority of investors I work with. They want to acquire properties below market, do some fixing, usually paint and carpet and some landscaping, and then list and sell for market value and pocket the profits.

There are three primary reasons to buy in the public auction space:

- The lowest price point in the market
- The fastest acquisition time
- Properties not found in the Multiple Listing Service (MLS)

There are also reasons why people don't make the effort to buy at the auction, and these often work in your favor!

I have been in the space for 16 years and I thought I had heard every excuse for not utilizing trustee sales, but every once in a while I am surprised. I was recently on a 'find it, fix it, and flip it' panel with a handful of my competitors. The audience was comprised of 185 real estate agents and brokers. One agent sitting in the first row asked, "Can you really buy at auction? I tried it for a week and didn't buy anything."

What was interesting to me, was one of those on the panel had just finished saying his strategy was door knocking. He said he knocks on 500 doors to find one 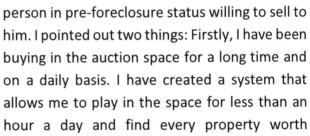 person in pre-foreclosure status willing to sell to him. I pointed out two things: Firstly, I have been buying in the auction space for a long time and on a daily basis. I have created a system that allows me to play in the space for less than an hour a day and find every property worth looking at. Secondly, it just takes patience and perseverance.

In Arizona for example, there can be up to six auctioneers at any given time crying out sales. They act of behalf of trustees, representing lenders (beneficiaries), who are charged with obtaining the highest bid possible. Sales held in Maricopa County, encompassing the greater Phoenix metro area, can be hectic to say the least. Conversely, I have personally witnessed and participated in sales in Tucson, San Diego, Los Angeles, Las Vegas, and Miami where the bidding process is much simpler and straight forward.

In some cases, you might be the only bidder. In other cases there may be a dozen people trying to bid on one property. The Phoenix metro area is large, in fact it's now the fifth largest city in the US, and there is a steady flow of auction properties being cried out on a daily basis. In 16 years, I have been the only bidder fewer than a dozen times. It's an amazing feeling to be the only one on top of a great deal. Chances are greater in smaller counties that investors and their agents will be the sole bidder more frequently and enjoy greater success in buying at greater profit too!

So what makes the perfect deal you don't want to miss? The most important factor will be your exit strategy, which we will be discussing again at greater length in Chapter 5. The opening bid amount in relation to the actual market value is also critical. Most important is how close the ultimate selling price will be in the 'sweet spot' of affordability to potential buyers.

This picture was taken at the Phoenix public auction. You can see our INFOclosure.com company shirts. We always made a point to look a little more professional than the rest of the crowd.

Where I deal, most investors are looking for a house that will sell for between $140,000 and $200,000 because they know these will sell fast as more buyers can afford them. When you find one of those sweet deals with a spread of around $30,000 between opening bid and actual market value, there will probably be more bidders than usual.

Upwards of $200,000 however, the sell cycle is longer, so even if there is a nice spread between opening bid and market value, the whole process will be lengthy. A lot of profit can get eaten up quickly in holding costs.

So there are many things to consider when you decide to invest in property at the foreclosure auction. To review, does acquisition cost and final sell price fit into the 'sweet spot' for your market? Don't forget factoring in your approximate rehab costs. And ... does it all jive with your exit strategy?

The 'sweet spot' concept is critical for anyone looking to do 'fix-and-flip'. The best way to determine the sweet spot is to consult several real estate professionals. Ask them what areas are hot and why they believe so. While it is true that every home will sell if it is priced right, you can stack the deck in your favor by leveraging what other professionals know. Look for areas where homes sell fast or with a low absorption rate which is determined by dividing the number of currently listed homes in an area by the three month running average of sold properties.

For example, take the number of homes for sale in an area, divided by the number of sold homes in that same area, and the result equals the absorption rate.

- ✓ 5 active homes for sale, divided by 5 average number of homes sold = 1, or an absorption rate of 1.
- ✓ When the absorption rate is less than 5 it's a seller's market.
- ✓ Between 5 and 7, it's a stable market
- ✓ Greater than 7, it's a buyer's market

Flippers are always looking for a seller's market. Investing consistently in a seller's market will boost your returns significantly. Turning your money three times a year or more is optimal.

After you know the ropes, you can make a lot of money at the foreclosure auction, but please know this:

A foreclosure auction is capitalism in its truest form. There are no guardrails and nothing to prevent you from making serious blunders. No one will care (but you) if you pay too much. No one will care if you lose money in the deal. The only protection is knowledge and experience. I'm going to try to give you that knowledge, which in itself is arming you with a lot more than most of those who show up at the auction.

If you take what I'm going to share with you here and add some experience, you will be a force to contend with. Many won't bid against you simply because you will know what you are doing and will have considered all the options before you step in to bid.

There is a psychology to bidding at an auction that can help you a great deal and that will be covered in Chapter 9. If you have played poker before, you will understand much of the psychological factors at play at the auction.

Paying For Your Winning Bid

Paying for an auction purchase varies from state to state. For example, here in Arizona you must hand the Trustee a cashier's check for $10,000 immediately upon a successful bid at the auction, and pay the remainder by 5 pm the next business day.

This fact alone might push out all but the wealthy from buying property at the auction, but there is an equalizer that can change things for the average investor, and that is hard money.

Hard money is a form of a bridge loan; a short term note that can be underwritten in one day. Unlike a conventional loan that takes weeks if not months to fund, a hard money loan is based more upon the value of the property rather than the creditworthiness of the person requesting the loan. So providing you made the $10,000 deposit with the Trustee, a hard money lender may give you the cash to acquire the property. Many 'fix-and-flip' investors I work with do this with every purchase they make. They pay interest only for the term of the loan, often 90 days for a fix-and-flip, and then sell the property, pay off the hard money loan and pocket the profit. We will talk much more about hard money in Chapter 10.

Hard money costs are just some of the holding costs you will have to pay from the date you acquire the property to when you sell if you are a fix-and-flip investor.

Here are some other expenses you will face:

- ✓ Utilities – Electric, gas, and other utilities
- ✓ Property taxes
- ✓ Up keep – landscaping, lawn mowing, watering plants, etc.
- ✓ Property Insurance
- ✓ Real estate commissions

- ✓ Legal fees
- ✓ New carpet and paint
- ✓ Other necessary repairs

So with this in mind, it becomes very clear how important the price of acquisition is compared to the actual market value of any property. That's what this book is about. This is an overview of buying foreclosed properties at public auction. Remember our favorite quote, 'the devil is in the details"? Nowhere is that more true than here.

So, are you beginning to see the possibilities? Great!

So now let's look at how you find these properties to bid on at auction. In addition, we'll examine how you arrive at your maximum bid in the next chapter.

Important Concepts

1. Consult a CPA.
2. Consult an attorney.
3. Commit to market study.

Chapter 3

Data Sourcing, Capture, and Management

"In God we trust. All others must bring data."

W. Edwards Deming

The very first time I appeared at a public auction, I realized I was truly a beginner in this space. Everyone had some form of a list they were working from and I quickly came to know the importance of getting my hands on a good source of data. The Phoenix area is quite large and there were a handful of companies to source data from. I began subscribing to these data services and showing up at auction to bid. Thinking I was a player, I soon realized I was still in the beginner box

Having your data organized and accessible is critical.

and my competition was bidding on properties that were not on my list. What I hadn't accounted for was postponed properties from previous days being rescheduled to the day I was there bidding. Talk about not knowing what you don't know! I have a strong sense of competition and pride and not having good or complete data drove me nuts. I went back to my data source and asked for the past 90 days' worth of data and began working it forward. It took me about 45 days to complete a very exhausting cleanup of the data sets, but finally I was able to show up at auction with complete and accurate information. Without it, I couldn't have called myself a real estate investor. It became very apparent that there was no service available that would

do every necessary task for me, as in gather and parse pertinent data, the ongoing updates to the data, and supporting market comparable studies, so I could accurately determine if there was really a deal. Having an entrepreneurial bent, I saw an opportunity in creating trusted and compiled data and providing it as a service, since none existed and didn't appear to be on the horizon.

There are multiple data or information sets you will need to be an effective player in this space.

Source Data: By this I mean the data gathered from notices of default, notices of trustee sale, or sheriffs' sale notice. This data is not complete in and of itself as you'll see in the example of an Arizona notice in the appendix section. While there is important information available there, much is missing.

Assessor Data: Source data will need to be scrubbed against either the county assessor's database, or a local multiple listing service (typically only available for licensed real estate agents). Scrubbing data needs to produce important items such as year built, square footage of house and lot, subdivision, number of bedrooms and bathrooms, property type, and whether there is a pool.

Market Comparable Data: I prefer to use the MLS. Again, this is only available to real estate agents. There are a few other sources such as Zillow where some basic comparable information is available, however the accuracy of third party sources like this can be questionable, once again bringing me back to the MLS. My preferred search in MLS encompasses everything within a one mile radius of the subject property, and sold in the last 90 days. I download the results into excel, then sort by "subdivision" as that is most relevant according to the appraiser community.

Auction Comparable Data: I added a level of data gathering that few of my competitors have even thought of. I am so often asked by clients considering buying in this space whether they have a chance at winning the property at the number they've arrived at. In response to this, I created what I call the "bid barometer", using the same criteria as Market

Original style of data used to buy at auction since 1998. This is an output from our current database through INFOclosure.com

Comparable Data. What this tells me is what third party bidders like myself paid at auction for a similar property. The benefit of knowing what has recently transacted at auction gives me more knowledge to intelligently re-examine my analysis before the auction begins. The time for this analysis of your potential deals is not when you are standing in front of the auctioneer. We will go more in depth when we cover the psychology of bidding in a later chapter.

Very few, if any, of the trustees or auctioneers supply data to investors. It seems counter intuitive given that the roll of the trustee is to get the most money possible for a property on behalf of their clients – the banks. It would make sense that they would supply investors with every possible bit of information to make an intelligent decision, but in fact, it's just the opposite.

This is a screen shot of our system that has evolved significantly in the past 16 years.

There are over 50 active trustees crying out sales in the Phoenix area. To obtain a list from each and try to work all the sale information effectively and quickly becomes an immense task. If you don't use a third party source, you'll need to mine the data yourself. You will need to pull information from the closest possible source, which is the country recorder. Every county without exception records the notices of foreclosure. Depending on your state, it may be called one of the following: *notice of default, notice of trustee sale, notice of sheriff sale,* or *notice of foreclosure.*

One thing I learned early on is that having good data attracts other investors who are interested in the space but not in doing the legwork. This is an opportunity for you to serve others and collect a fee for service. Whether I like to admit it or not, I have evolved into a bit of a data junky. Numbers don't lie and buying at auction is not emotional, so I have to rely on numbers, and good ones at that. I have created an elaborate database to support buying at auction. We call it SOURCE 3.0 and it is a true, custom written database. In the early days, I used excel, but that falls woefully short of being able to manage large data sets and sustain accuracy.

Important Concepts

1. Find the data closest to the source.
2. Manage with a database.
3. Identify opportunity to share and monetize it.

Chapter 4

Showing Up and Observing

"Nothing has such power to broaden the mind as the ability to investigate systematically and truly all that comes under thy observation in life."

Marcus Aurelius

Prior to making my first bid, I knew I needed to get the lay of the land. I decided to attend an auction and first observe. Everything researched and read about the public auction space said there was no welcoming committee and they were RIGHT! Like other novices before me, I looked through several "notices of trustee sale" and found a common address. "201 W Jefferson"

Observe, learn, take notes, and then go for it.

was the common thread and is the location of our county court house in Phoenix. So with this address safely in hand I ventured downtown, found a parking spot, and approached the court house. I showed up early because I really wanted to see the auction process from the very beginning to the end. I entered the court house main doors and proceeded to go through security. This was prior to 9/11, but you still had to empty pockets and take your belt off. The Maricopa county court house is a large facility so I continued down hall after hall looking for the place where they held the public auctions. After many passes up one hall and down another I knew I had to do the unthinkable and ask for directions. Much to my dismay, every person I asked gave me a *"what are you talking about?"* look. Feeling a bit deflated, I decided to head back home and re-group. Obviously there was a lot I still needed to learn. As I exited the building I looked over to my right and saw a small group of people gathered around one individual. This was a very nondescript setting. No signs, no shirts with logos, and no apparent information. No real surprise that it was dominated by people in t-shirts, shorts, and flip flops. Seeing this I knew I was home! I approached slowly and stayed a safe distance and just listened. This was back in 1998, and what I observed was a group of people who seemed to know exactly what they were doing.

There is no welcoming committee! In fact the serious players get very grumpy when you show up and let you know it. The pros don't even see you. It's sort of like taking a seat at a poker game and the other players hope you have no idea what you are doing. They're going to give you that 'get lost' look.

That's the bad news! The good news is that if you hang around a while and know what you're doing, you will get a grudging respect from the other bidders. The 'regulars' may even nod to you on occasion as a greeting. From the beginning, I made it a rule not to associate or get personal with the competition. I am an introvert by nature, so not engaging in conversation never bothers me. Extroverts beware! At its core, the extrovert needs to be in conversation. It fosters and supports their very character. I am not saying that being an extrovert is bad

Las Vegas public auction.

or wrong in any way, just putting out the warning that this characteristic can lead to getting sucked into the competitions hand. (I really am not trashing extroverts.) In short, there is no better teacher than experience; watching how others play the game. I would show up and watch for hours before I ever got into active bidding. There are procedures and protocols you will pick up quickly, and there may be half a dozen trustees selling on any given day, each with their own way of doing things.

Here's a small check list for your auction visits:

- o Identify the auctioneers crying the sales.
- o Determine if there is more than one auction taking place simultaneously. (In Phoenix we can have up to 5 or 6 auctions happening at the same time.)
- o Observe the sign-in procedure.
- o Observe the way in which the sales are cried. (It will seem confusing at first, but listen closely and you will follow the process easily.)
- o Observe how each auctioneer conducts a sale and allows or requires the bidders to participate. The auctioneer/trustee has some discretion

within the governing laws on how to conduct sales. There very well may be some differences from one auctioneer to another and differences from county to county.

- o Watch how the auctioneer ends an auction and takes the last bid. (I'll share some bidding techniques in chapter 9)
- o Understand the flow of money and what is required.
- o Observe when the auctions start and when they end. Showing up late to an auction and asking for a sale to be reopened because of a traffic delay will not carry any weight. Show up early and stay late.

Note: You might find what looks like favoritism toward the regulars at auction. For instance, to qualify to bid in Phoenix, the bidder must show a $10,000 cashier's check. We, the regulars, have it made out to ourselves and sign it over to the trustee once we are the successful bidder. New bidders are not allowed to do that until such time the auctioneer decides they're "OK" and will accept a check made out to themselves. Again, this is not illegal, but falls within the discretion of the auctioneer/trustee and within the governing laws of the state.

Chances are, if you choose to deal in a large county, you'll see the same trustees and bidders all the time. You will very soon learn who the players are and know which trustee represents the property you want.

When there are multiple auctioneers, you'll need to discover which trustees they are crying for. It is nothing short of heart breaking to be standing at one table waiting for a sale when your competition is buying that same property at another table 20 feet away. Here in Arizona, eight auctioneers represent two or three hundred different trustees. Staying late and asking the auctioneer what trustees they represent is an important early step for anyone contemplating this game. On the other hand, consider a city like Las Vegas where all sales are conducted by only one auctioneer (Nevada Legal News) at 10am each morning. The process is very simple and easy to follow.

It's important to know how and when to approach an auctioneer. Let me start by saying that auctioneers are hired by the trustee to conduct the sale on their behalf. These folks are human, and often under paid for the work they do. With that said, they can sometimes not be the most pleasant people to work with. In their defense, they have to put up with a great deal: rude bidders, egos the size of Texas, newbies asking endless questions while they're trying to conduct business. So, what's the best way to approach them? I found that showing up early and observing is good for other purposes, but I leave the auctioneers alone so they can get set up to do business. I found that waiting until sales are over is the best time to ask questions. I did find one exception to that rule. There was one auctioneer that would answer any question prior to auction, but then would completely ignore me after the sales were cried.

You really never quite know exactly what you'll experience on any given day.

This is a good time to back up and create clarity regarding some of the important players. First, the beneficiary is the party carrying the note (the lender) and needs to satisfy the bad debt via the auction process. It should be noted that in every state, there are specific laws providing protection to the home owner, or trustor, while allowing the party owed to either be made whole or take the property back. A common misconception is that the bank has control of the property going into the foreclosure process. They do not.

Second is the trustee. This entity is hired by the beneficiary to facilitate the auction process and make their investment whole. In Arizona and most of the western states, we use a "deed of trust" as the security instrument for the loan along with a promissory note. Under the remedies section of a deed of trust, the trustee is listed so it is known in advance who will conduct the foreclosure process in the event of a default.

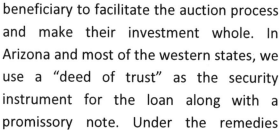

Third is the auctioneer who is hired by the trustee to cry the sale. In most cases, the trustee is out of state and does not cry the sale directly. In all states, the law requires that sales are held in a public place. No one can charge admittance fees and anyone can come and observe. The regulars will make you feel like you shouldn't be there, but that's part of the strategy. Keep your game-face on!

The Opening Bid

The beneficiary determines the opening bid which is the least amount they will accept for a property. Sometimes in the daily auction record, you'll see the winning bid as $150,001, for example. The 'and one dollar' at the end of a winning bid usually means there was only one person interested in that piece of property, and they bid $1 over the opening.

I am often asked how the beneficiary comes up with their opening bid. Before I tackle that, I want to pause for a moment and share a few thoughts. I often hear people say, "There are no good deals at an auction." As you already know, I'm a 16 year veteran of public auctions. The people who make money consistently in this area are those who show up every day to play. For these past 16 years, on any given day, about two thirds of the opening bids are too high priced for me to bid on and those properties usually don't sell, revert back to the beneficiary and become 'REO' (bank owned) properties. That's a lot of properties going back to the bank! Does that mean I should fold my tent and go home? Absolutely not. It means that I will find the best properties out of what is left. Consistency and persistence will make you successful in this space and in just about anything else in life.

Back to task... How does the beneficiary arrive at their opening bid? The best explanation that I've heard and believe to be true is a specific formula they apply to each area the subject property is located in whether it is by zip code, city, county or state. They calculate what it will take to get the property off their books in the event no one bids. They have to determine if such a situation will result in a loss. If the possibility of a loss exists, they consider taking the loss at the time of the auction or taking the property back and managing the loss later.

Other considerations are the current condition of the property as well as the surrounding area. The beneficiary will order a BPO (broker price opinion) prior to the auction providing them with a comparable study  for the property, marketing information that will help in the decision making process, and information on the surrounding area as to whether it is appreciating or declining. One thing to keep in mind is that banks are not in the business of managing properties. Those with real estate holdings on their books consider this to adversely affect their ability to get money from the Federal Reserve. So the banks have a big decision to make when determining opening bids.

Part of the analysis also includes what they currently have on the books in that surrounding area. If they have too many, they will set an opening bid low enough to ensure they will not get it back. If the opposite is true and their existing inventory is low, they may keep the opening bid high in order to take it back. This baffles many new comers as they do not understand the banks position regarding that particular property. A beneficiary has the right to get back the unpaid principle balance as well as any late fees, penalties etc., which legally apply. An opening bid by the beneficiary which includes everything they are entitled to is called a "credit bid". When a bank decides they don't want a property back and a credit bid would need to be too high to incent other higher bids, they will take their loss at the time of the sale. Reducing a credit bid to an amount to entice bidding is referred to as a "specified bid". Once again, this is the beneficiary taking a loss at the time of sale and skipping the hassles of taking it back and managing it to incur an even greater loss.

The Trustee will not accept any bid lower than the opening bid, but that doesn't mean you can't get that property eventually at a lower price. If no one bids on the foreclosed property, the property reverts back to the beneficiary. After the bank is in possession of the property, people are free to make any offer they want to the bank. There are many investors who employ this strategy! Personally, I have never employed this tactic because it's simply too difficult. Buying direct from auction is much easier and faster. I'm not saying there isn't profit to be made, just that the effort to acquire the property is much greater than bidding at auction and taking immediate possession. Summing up, the larger the bank the harder it is to buy directly from them. Smaller banks and individuals may be easier to work with. Again, this is strategy unto itself and not for the novice investor.

Some investors will make a list of all properties that did not sell at auction. These investors believe that if no one was interested, the bank knows that they will have to sell them for a lesser amount. Banks make lousy property managers and hate the costs they must pay to maintain the property. Utilities must remain turned on, they must take care of landscaping, and pay any other repairs that are necessary. Therefore they're motivated to unload these properties and may accept a much lower bid.

I and the many clients I work with, have chosen to avoid this route. We want fast acquisition and there is nothing faster than public auction. If you place the winning bid, you own it right away.

This is the best time to bring up an important topic, and that is illegal activities that sometimes happen at auction locations. This topic is critical and must be understood by all investors entering the space of public auction. The first is called collusion. Collusion is the act of two or more parties working together in an effort to purchase the property at auction for less than what it would normally have been bid to. Let's clarify this further. It has happened to me on several occasions over the years. A regular pulls me aside and says something like "Rick, are you bidding on "xyz" property?" I answer that I might be. He says he needs to buy something for his brother in-law and "xyz" is a prefect property for him. "If you don't bid against me, I won't bid against you on the next one." Fortunately I am often bidding on behalf of a client, so my response is always easy. "I am bidding for a client and will be bidding regardless of who you are bidding for." Even if I had been there for myself, I would still bid. I don't extend favors at auction, nor should you. While this may seem harmless to anyone being offered it for the first time, it carries serious consequences. The act of that "favor" is a class six felony.

Forms of collusion do not stop there and is why making "friends" with the competition never works out. With or without specific relationships, you may be offered money (bribery) not to bid against an individual. There are typically one or two players that believe they control all the buying at auction and in many ways it appears they do. If they're paying or receiving money for a manipulation of bidding, they're acting illegally.

One of several traps for an unsuspecting new investor to avoid is being quietly offered a sum of money not to bid on a property. It appears harmless, but what they don't realize is that the same person will prey on them going forward. The next time the new investor bids and wins a property, that same guy walks up and says, I didn't big against you on that so now you owe me. Before they know it, they're caught in a trap they can't get out of and have most often broken the law. Remember, money doesn't have to change hands for an action to be illegal. Two or more parties working together manipulating the bid is the illegal act.

Fortunately I have always been able to avoid getting involved with collusion. Would I like to buy properties cheaper at auction? Sure, but not at the risk of ruining my reputation or going to jail. I remember a few years back when a relatively new regular started to play the game. He asked me if I was going to bid on a particular property when it appeared we were the only two bidders. He made his offer, but I politely declined. Later that day I ran into him at another auction and out of the blue he came up to me and blurted out "I think you misunderstood me this morning". Keep in mind I had not spoken to him at all other than politely declining his offer. I could hear the group that he retreated to behind me whispering, "Don't ask him, he won't play." There was a sense of nervousness from those around me. I was and am proud of the reputation I created for myself around being a straight player at auction.

The question you might be thinking is, what of it? I want properties cheaper and who is getting harmed? There are two parties that get harmed when a property does not sell at a fair, competitive price. The first is the beneficiary who has the legal right to collect all of their unpaid principle as well as late fees and costs. The second party harmed is the trustor or home owner prior to the auction. Funds over and above the winning bid belong to the trustor. Most people being foreclosed upon have no idea these funds belong to them. This is also the place where other legitimate lienholders have a right to claim debts owed them before the trustor. Other groups that might have a claim are second position lien holders, HOA's, general or sub-contractors who haven't been paid – just to name a few. I am very familiar with this process as I created a company in 2004 that works with home owners to claim excess proceeds after auction. The largest check I assisted in returning to a client was $212,000. This is a legal process and takes considerable time, as well as attorney services to perform, yet very rewarding. We just recently began to work excess proceeds again in 2014 as higher amounts of excess equity is becoming more common again.

Just as every county in the US may have different locations where auctions are held and different payment requirements, they may also each have their own 'personalities'. Different players can create a very different environment!

In Phoenix, the auction is held outdoors, literally right on the county courthouse steps, rain or shine! Fortunately in Phoenix it's almost always shine. If you're ever in the Phoenix area, I would like to invite you to 201 W. Jefferson St., downtown Phoenix on any weekday at 10am. You will find my bidders in our  company uniform shirts displaying the INFOclosure.com logo. Feel free to get a list of that day's properties and ask them any question you may have.

It's easy to feel intimidated at first, but just like poker you need to develop and show up with a game face.

Only you can determine what that is or looks like. I always maintain a pleasant, cordial, but aloof approach. Negativity in any form never serves your end game. But trust me on this: after you have attended a couple of weeks' worth of auctions, you'll begin to understand how it works, who the players are, how to make your bids, etc.

This is the background effort you need to make, even if you use a third-party service like mine to do the bidding for you. Every employee I hire in my business has to spend a few days at the auction shadowing an experienced bidder before they do anything else.

Buying in the space of public auction is the most powerful way to acquire properties. Nowhere else can I analyze a property today, bid on it tomorrow, and literally take possession the following day. In my opinion it is still the lowest price point in the market, and it is inventory not found on MLS. (Multiple Listing Service).

Important Concepts

1. Observe at least one full week before playing.
2. Identify competition and auctioneers.
3. Start planning on how you are going to show up (game face).

Chapter 5

The Players and the Competition

"I have been up against tough competition all my life. I wouldn't know how to get along without it."

Walt Disney

There are a variety of people you will meet at auction and just as many reasons they're there. Of course, the main goal of just about everyone is to get a great deal on a property or home, something below the actual market value.

Beyond that, there are certain types you will start to see, and they come in a few recognizable groups. Let's take a look at some of these folks and the roles they play.

Knowing the players give you the edge in the game.

The Trustee/Auctioneer

The Trustee is the party managing the property disposition on behalf of the beneficiary. The Trustee is appointed by the holder of the note that is in default. Often this manager's sole responsibility, according to law, is to offer the property at auction and award it to the party making the highest bid. The Trustee also takes possession of funds from the winning bidder and, in turn, pays the bank their due proceeds, with any excess going to the county. How this happens varies by state and in some instances the bidder must pay the full amount immediately on winning the bid. In other states, only a partial deposit is required at win time with the balance due at a later time. In Arizona, the winning bidder must pay the Trustee a deposit of $10,000 immediately and the balance the next business day. California and Nevada require the full amount immediately. Know the rules for your state!

The Auctioneer is normally an employee of an auctioneering service, engaged by the Trustee to physically cry the sales. They are the individuals that can make a huge difference in the dynamics of any particular auction and would be well to get to know. Some are expert at what they do and others are just the opposite. The sole purpose of the trustee is to protect the interests of the beneficiary and get the most money possible for the subject property. With that said, there are many occasions where I felt the auctioneer representing the trustee did not rise to this responsibility. Often rushing through sales or not crying out in a loud enough voice did not allow all interested parties a chance to participate. While it is true that investors need to be ready at all times, the auctioneers and trustees sometimes don't put in the required effort to secure the highest bid.

Professional Bidders

These are the people who bid on behalf of other investors and are usually easy to spot. They often have one or more cell phones plastered to their ear, relaying real time information to their clients about the status of a bid. Pro bidders always know beforehand the high bid

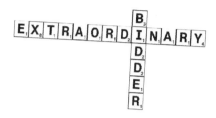

amount their client is willing to pay, even though the client may go higher in a competitive situation, necessitating constant real-time communication. This is the advantage of using a professional bidding service. There is no emotion here, as the pros are playing with someone else's money. The investor determines how much he is willing to bid and if it goes higher, he bows out and lets the other guy have it.

My company, INFOclosure.com, performs this service for many investors. Our clients keep on deposit with us the $10,000, which is the minimum the Trustee will accept as a deposit in Phoenix. We are present daily at every auction location and perform the actual bidding. Our professional bidders stay in constant phone contact with our clients during the process.

All of our bidders are also licensed real estate agents. You must check with your state laws to determine whether a third-party bidder is required to have a real estate license.

As I said earlier, our pro bidders always wear a uniform shirt and ball cap sporting the INFOclosure.com logo. This lets the auctioneer know they are dealing with a pro who knows what they're doing. It also serves the purpose of letting other bidders know the same!

Investors

At every auction, there are do-it-yourself investors attending and bidding. Often these investors are relatively new to the game or only buy one or two properties a year to supplement their income. They tend to be most interested in properties that are relatively close to where they live.

This is where I got my start in real estate investing; what I consider to be my true start. What I quickly realized was that my time was best spent analyzing deals coming up and overseeing the projects I had going. Taking time to physically go to auction and bid was not the best use of my time. This is something I could train someone to do. Being an entrepreneur, I saw early on the need for investors to have a single source of data, pre-auction due diligence, and bid execution. It was clear to me why so many investors stay out of this space. None of the "dots" are connected as in traditional real estate, and what you don't know can hurt you. I was looking for that service, realized there wasn't one, and proceeded to create it with the intent of serving investor clients.

Once they start to buy multiple properties, they end up using a service like INFOclosure.com. When they become 'professional investors', they can't possibly 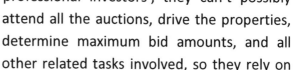 attend all the auctions, drive the properties, determine maximum bid amounts, and all other related tasks involved, so they rely on companies like mine to do a lot of the heavy lifting. I work with several investors who buy more than 30 properties every year and couldn't succeed without our help. After all, investors want or already have financial independence and don't want to work 60 hours a week doing research and actually spending hours at auctions!

The Amateur vs The Casual Investor

These guys are so easy to spot! Often they look confused and perplexed by what's happening around them. There are no handbooks or guides handed out that explain the chaos. (That's why I'm writing this book!)

Often there are multiple auctions set up in one location and amateurs don't know who's handling the property they're interested in. Foreclosure auction is not a friendly place. It's all business and it's not in anyone's best interest to help you!

Downtown Phoenix public auction.

If the competition appears to be interested in you, BEWARE!

To all the pros and experienced investors, these amateurs are competition and are thought of as irritants that may drive a bid up too high or make other mistakes not conducive to their success.

It's not unlike casino poker. If you get into a game with serious players and make rookie mistakes, the regulars will soon prey on your lack of skill. I recall one of the worst and most blatant mistakes made by a novice real estate agent trying to buy a property for her client. She arrived and right away began talking with every competitor about the subject property. She had never been to the auction before and didn't know what she didn't know. She was exposing her hand to the other players. I felt so bad that I pulled her aside and told her to stop blowing her own deal. To serve her client properly, she needed to keep quiet. Fortunately for her and her client, the sale postponed. I let her know what a blessing that was for her. She was very appreciative and ended up using our company to bid the next time the property came up for sale.

Ironically, this is one of the ways I built my business in the early days of my investing career. I would look for these people (there were many and they weren't hard to spot) and offer some understanding about what was going on. Then I'd tell them that I would be standing around if they had any more questions. Within a couple of minutes they would usually come back to me and ask a lot more questions! I introduced the concepts of how to pick the best properties and how to determine the right bid, and let them know that I could bid on their behalf for a fee if they were interested.

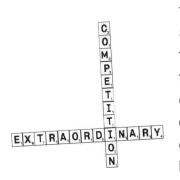

I got a lot of clients that way. And as my business grew, many of these investors grew in their confidence and experience and let my company handle all their transactions.

The Competition

In many instances there is only a single bidder, so in effect there is no competition. In such a situation, the savvy bidder offers one dollar over the opening bid. Every time I see auction results with a property that sold for a price like $120,001, for example, I know there was only one bidder who bid just a buck over the opening amount.

At other times, especially places where property values are on the rise in highly desirable areas, the competition can be fierce with a half dozen bidders or more.

The competition for properties rises in areas where the buyer knows they will be able to sell the property fast after the fixing and repairs that need to be made are completed, or the opening bid is far below the actual market value and in an area that is considered affordable for the average person.

In the Phoenix market where I primarily operate, houses priced in the $150's or thereabouts sell quickly and easily. When an opening bid is $110,000 to $120,000, many bidders are attracted and often bids are driven up to the point where no profit is possible.

Some of those bidding are actually looking for their own primary residence, so the big spread an investor needs to make an acceptable profit is not their motivation. They may be very happy to get a home for a higher price which then drives the typical investor out of the bidding process.

My best advice is to use my Maximum Bid Sheet (Appendix 1) and don't go more than that amount. Remember, there is often someone willing to make less profit than you are. Know how much profit you need to end up with for the effort to be worthwhile. You'll be spending time, money, and incur holding costs on the property, so don't bid more than an amount that will allow you to make that profit.

I can't tell you how many reasons I have heard for not buying at auctions. One of the most common is that "buyers are paying market price". While there are homes that go higher than I would consider paying, not all of them sell that high. Being patient and playing every day is the key to success in picking up properties that are right for you. If every real estate agent quit the game because they couldn't find their client the home of their dreams there would be a lot of people out of the business. People get outbid regularly when they are looking for the home of their dreams, but don't stop. They keep going until they find what they want.

The nice thing about the auction is it happens every day, and another fantastic deal is just around the corner.

Important Concepts

1. Avoid making friends at auction.
2. Identify the competition early.
3. Identify who you can serve.

Chapter 6

Hard Money

I was actively buying in the space of public auction for about a year when I ran into a friend I had lost touch with who had left corporate America a year before I did. He had gone into hard money lending while I had gone the fix-and-flip route. Up to that point, I had been paying cash for my auction purchases and had enough to buy 3 or 4 homes depending on the purchase price.

You don't know what you don't know.

Again, this was a situation where I didn't know what I didn't know. I was unaware of the concept of hard money lending and how I could take what I had and leverage it to continue to make extraordinary profits from these ordinary auctions in a much bigger way.

Because I feel so strongly now about hard money and its relationship to the auction space, I knew I had to add a chapter about it in this book. Understanding it, sourcing it, knowing how to calculate it, and how to leverage it for additional profits is what I want to focus on.

66

Understanding how to source and use 'hard money' can make a huge difference in your real estate investing endeavors. Unless you have nearly unlimited amounts of cash, you need to understand how savvy investors, even those who have a lot of cash, still use hard money in their strategy.

Hard money is the great 'equalizer', if you will. If the only bidders were those with enough cash to pay in full for properties, investing in real estate would have remained a sport only the very rich could participate in. Fortunately for you and me, that isn't the case today.

In the simplest terms, hard money is cash available from private lenders. These lenders lend money to investors, and the loans are collateralized by the properties they buy. If an investor fails to pay on the loan as promised, the lender can foreclose on the property just as in conventional lending.

Because these loans come from private individuals, there are far fewer regulations to contend with and they can be funded in one day. Hard money lenders come in two flavors. First there are private individuals that have cash available and are willing to lend you the money for your deal. Then there are bona fide

and licensed hard money lenders that comply with state regulations, which give you some level of protection as a borrower. As I stated earlier, hard money is lightly regulated and private individuals typically lend without any regulation. Which is better? I would recommend whenever possible to work with a licensed entity. Typically, licensed hard money lenders are lending their own funds and money from other registered investment pools. You are not a big fish in their pond, but just another normal client. I've seen situations where the borrower gets a call from their private individual lender asking them to pay off the loan early or refinance it with someone else due to some occurrence in their life, such as a divorce or some other urgent need for cash. This doesn't support a very professional transaction and won't happen with a licensed lender. When leveraging borrowed money, always use a licensed entity that provides protection by the state governing body.

With a conventional bank originated loan, there are reams of paperwork involved. You are given a list of documents you must provide to prove your ability to repay the loan, appraisals must be obtained, and then the entire package must be sent to an underwriting department who makes sure everything is in order, and makes the decision for or against funding the loan. Then the documents go to a title company who schedules the closing. After you sign all the documents at the closing, it takes up to another day or so for the actual funds to be transferred and you get handed the keys to the house. This entire process can take 2 months or more!

At the foreclosure auction, you must pay the entire amount anywhere from immediately to a couple of days, depending on the state you buy in, so this doesn't work. You need a money source that can make its decision immediately and fund the loan before the deadline required by the Trustee.

The hard money lender doesn't care as much about you, the borrower. They care about the market value of the property, and the loan to value ratio.

Most hard money lenders will require that the investor put down 20% to 30% of the amount needed to acquire the property. That way, if they were forced to foreclose, there is sufficient equity enabling them to sell the property and make their money back, including all penalties, attorney fees, and any other fees involved in the event of default and foreclosure.

So why doesn't everybody use hard money to buy a house? These loans are designed to be short term bridge loans of three to six months. Interest rates are much higher than conventional loans from traditional lenders. How high are the interest rates? As I write this in the early part of 2015, the normal interest rates for hard money are from 16% – 20%, and zero to 6 points. Typically the higher the rate, the lower the points, if any. We have both a 16% and an 18% no point structure in our hard money company, Titan Capital Holdings.

So how does an investor use this hard money in their investment strategy?

For the fix-and-flip investor, hard money loans are used to acquire the property at the auction. Their monthly payment is interest only for the term of the loan or the length of time it is used. So if an investor plans to do some repair and cosmetic enhancements and then sell immediately, she may take a hard money loan for 3 months, paying interest only for exact number of days the loan is used. When the property sells, the hard money lender is paid back from the proceeds.

I have used this in my own foreclosure investing activities, even when I have the cash to buy the property in full. The interest expense for my use of hard money funds is just that, an expense I figure into the holding costs of the property. Remember, I am only using the hard money cash for a short period of time, often less than three months, and as I am paying interest only, it's in reality a small expense when compared to the amount of profit I carefully planned to make when I sell. So often new investors are shocked when they hear 18% interest on a six month note. It is in fact really inexpensive money given that it performs in a space where conventional financing cannot play. Banks are not equipped to lend same day or next day for purchases at an auction. The key to getting the right terms for your deal is based on your exit strategy. If you are a fix-and-flipper, typically a six month note is sufficient. Stay with a no-points option and the rate becomes less important. An 18% rate never scares me.

Another consideration is risking my own capital. Although I plan and have always paid as required for my hard money borrowing, if the worst happened I have only risked the 20% to 30% I put down. In very rare scenarios like a total market collapse or some other calamity, if I had paid entirely with my own money, I could lose far more.

The other type of investor who makes good use of hard money is the buy and hold investor. These investors plan to rent the property they acquire for a period of time, and then sell when appreciation does its magic  and the property is worth more than it is today. They want the rent they receive to either be positive cash flow or break even every month, betting on the appreciation to be their big pay day sometime down the road. In areas of rapid appreciation, this strategy works well, and I know several investors who have made millions doing this.

For the buy-and-hold investors, hard money plays a critical role in buying at auction and elsewhere. Long term investors will ultimately use conventional financing to take out the hard money loan after the purchase. The hard money allows them to make a successful immediate purchase that would not happen but for their ability to leverage hard money. They simply refinance the property into a conventional loan once they have acquired the property.

Timing is the crucial concern here, and the risks are greater in my way of thinking. I know many who were caught up in the pre-bust period of the early to mid-2000s, buying up everything in sight, betting on the dizzying upward spiral of prices like it was never going to end.

Well, end it did! And many of these people lost their shirts as well as all their money. One investor I know, bought six condos in Las Vegas for $200,000 each in 2006. The salesperson told her that in one year the properties would be worth $350,000, and they had the statistics of past performance to back that up.

Then the crash happened. The anticipated profits collapsed. Within another year, these condos were selling at foreclosure auction for $70,000 each. Millions in investments evaporated in a few short months. Thousands in the Southwest – Phoenix, Las Vegas, Southern California, and other places were forced to walk away from properties and faced bankruptcy.

After this massive correction in the housing industry played itself out, some of the hardest hit areas in terms of depreciation started rebounding as fast as they had fallen. Investors who bought on that side of the housing crisis made a lot of money! In places like Las Vegas and Phoenix the property values shot upward of 28% or more seemingly overnight.

It's all about the timing.

Where I live in the Phoenix area prices have leveled off somewhat. Appreciation is still happening here, but not at the meteoric rate of a year ago.

As they say, one man's misfortune is another man's opportunity. During the crash of 2007 – 2008, there was a glut of foreclosed properties for sale at the auction. There were bargains every day, so much so that hedge funds entered the fray and started buying hundreds of properties a day. Most of that is over now as we returned to a normal market, but there are still plenty of bargains available every day. Understanding hard money and how to use it to your advantage is critical to your success as a real estate investor.

Finding a hard money lender is not difficult. No, they don't advertise, but you can get a name and a phone number by talking with a realtor, or calling a title company and asking them. If you hint that you might be using them as the title company when you buy a property, they will give you this information freely.

Knowing how to crunch the numbers is important and I want to outline the basics so you are ready to go when the opportunity for a buy arises.

With an 18% interest rate, divide .18 by 360, giving you the daily factor of .0005, from here you can calculate daily and monthly interest. Just multiply the total estimated number of days you're going to use the loan by .0005. Take for example a loan amount of $100,000. $100,000 multiplied by .0005 is $50 – that is $50 per day of interest, or $1500 per month. It's very easy to calculate and now you know.

Developing a good relationship with a hard money lender will really help you in the long run. I have done many deals with a few specific lenders, and always paid them according to contract. Now, I can just call one of them anytime and tell them I have a property I want to acquire. They tell me to go ahead, they will cover the balance. The approval is almost automatic, and sometimes they will let me get by with less than 20% down. They know me, know how successful I have been, and they understand from past experience that they risk very little in funding my deals.

It takes time and experience to develop that kind of relationship, but it's worth it. Knowing that you can get funded with a minimum of questions and red tape makes you more confident and successful as an investor in foreclosed property at auctions.

Be aware: In 2009, just after the crash, hard money in the Phoenix area was difficult to come by. I had many clients trying to buy at auction but could not find hard money. Out of necessity I created my own hard money company and today we are licensed in three different states and growing. It is an exciting part of my overall business model. We operate under the name of Titan Capital Holdings.

Things to be aware of with respect to hard money

1. Read all documents carefully!
2. Be aware of late fees and extension fees if you haven't sold by the end of the loan's term.
3. Be aware of accelerating interest rates if and when they apply.
4. Be aware of verbiage that could necessitate putting additional money down if there is a change in market value.

Hard money isn't hard if you plan ahead. I've always said the time to look for a hard money lender is not when you need one. Experienced real estate investors run into deals sometimes that need to close quickly. Having a relationship set up is critical to your overall success as an investor. Don't lose profit or kill a deal because you can't pull financing together. Hard money lenders are waiting for your call and want to do business with you. The more experienced and professional you are, the more they're going to want to do business with you. You create fear or confidence in the heart of your hard money lender by how you do business. Show up professionally.

Important Concepts

1. Hard money lenders are a valued part of your team.
2. Hard money is for short term loans only.
3. Get to know several hard money lenders <u>before</u> you need one.

Chapter 7

Analyzing the Deal & Creating the Bid

"Get the habit of analysis — analysis will in time enable synthesis to become your habit of mind."

Frank Lloyd Wright

We mentioned earlier that occasionally there will be only one bidder for a particular property. However, it would be a BIG mistake to assume that $1 over the opening bid is always a good deal!

This is capitalism, pure and simple. The holder of the note on the foreclosed property wants to recover as much as possible, but they also know that if there are

Analysis is the biggest determinant for profit.

no bidders, they get the property back, and it becomes 'REO', that is "real estate owned", or "bank owned".

Of all the money that is made or lost in foreclosure investing, nothing is a bigger determinant than the way you analyze the deal and create your maximum bid. I have seen some of the smartest investors make errors in their analysis that tanked the deal before they even got started.

In 1999, I was able to avoid a very big mistake. I had been buying less than a year and had successfully purchased about 10 houses. Being a single father of two and always in a rush to get them off to school and down to auctions in time, I did a lot of my analysis on the fly. On this particular day, I took my position to bid as the property I was interested in was being called out. I remember a feeling of impending disaster settle into the pit of my stomach. I've had this feeling at other times in my life and it has served me well as a warning.

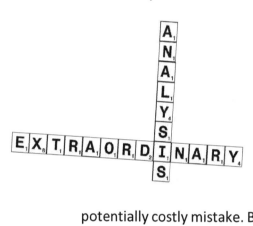

I stepped back and looked again at my numbers on this particular sale. I realized quickly that I had not factored in profit to my numbers. I quickly recalculated my numbers and stepped back into the game, avoiding a potentially costly mistake. Being a reasonably intelligent guy, I realized I needed to create a tool that would allow me to account for all those known costs and factors that come up in every deal. That day I went home and created what I call the "Max Bid Sheet", seen in Appendix 1. This is a very basic and straight forward tool I use to this day in buying property. With everything we have going on in our minds, we need a tool such as this to reduce the possibility of human error.

Of course every investor knows the old adage, "buy low and sell high". When all is said and done, that's what an investor wants to do.

But how do you ensure that the bid you determine as your maximum will ensure a low enough acquisition cost enabling you to sell high enough for the profit you want?

The key is in your analysis, and conservatively looking at all potential expenses related to buying and owning the property. This is where my 'Max Bid Sheet', attached in the appendix of this book, comes into play.

There are both variable and fixed costs to consider when analyzing a good buy at auction. Two of the most fluctuating variables are market value and repairs, so let me start with them.

Let's begin with market value (MV). There is no shame in asking for help to determine your exit price on a flip deal. So many people don't or won't, and it can cost them a ton of money at every turn. Choose a MV that's too high, and you end up chasing the market down, sometimes selling for less than it's worth, thereby losing out on profit and even possibly a loss of capital invested. I use MLS almost exclusively to determine my exit price. Here's my formula:

I map a one mile radius around the subject property.

I use a square footage range 20% higher and lower than my subject property.

I export the information into excel. Our MLS gives us all the related column headings which allows me to sort and compare data with ease rather than flipping through hard copy MLS print-outs for comparable properties. Once I have my data exported the fun begins.

I sort first by "status" and then by "subdivision". The status sort allows me to separate all the active listings (my competition) and the "closed" sales (my comparable), and lastly group the "pending" sales. Pending sales is the tricky one in that you don't know the actual contract price until it closes. I typically look at the "days on market" figure, but I will share more about that later.

I am going to reframe this market value concept again because it is so important. Now I have my comps broken down by status and subdivision. I am most concerned with comparables within the subdivision. FHA appraisers are looking for "model match" comparables in the same subdivision within the last 90 days. If they can't find any, their next move is to look at comparables within the subdivision in the past six months, from there they will go to those within a one mile radius and six months out. It gets complex after that! So, if you want to reduce your risk and give yourself the best chance at success, treat this process as carefully and as exacting as professional appraisers do.

Here are some other factors in comparing that you need to consider. Two story houses comp for less per square foot than single story homes. If your subject property is a two story house and all your comparables are single story, your resulting price per square foot will not be accurate. (It's cheaper to build up.) Next, in-ground pools, very popular in the west and southern states, play a big role depending on the design and size. Be careful if your subject property is without a pool and your comparable properties have them. The number of bedrooms also has an effect one direction or another. Depending on the property you're looking at, you could see a $2500 to $5000 increase in value due to an extra bedroom. I always like to deal with properties that have a minimum of three bedrooms. Anytime you get more, that's a bonus! Lastly, you need to consider carports and garages. Depending on where you are in the country, you may find houses with attached garages. Historically though, many older homes were built with carports only. Again, make sure you are comparing apples to apples whenever possible.

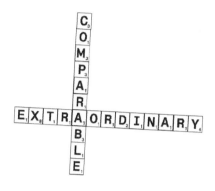

The next variable component is repairs. I literally could write an additional book on how to estimate repairs. It is always the most important question new investors ask as well as their biggest concern, and rightfully so. I break single family homes into two categories: "sweeps" and "everything else". A sweep is a house that is seven years old or newer. With respect to repairs it needs very little; a fresh coat of paint, carpet, light landscaping, and a good cleaning and you are ready to go to market. Typical costs are $6000 or less for a sweep. Mind you, that number is a target.

As for "everything else", repair costs will ultimately depend on original construction and year built. In Arizona for example, I typically stay away from homes built before 1955. Remember, Arizona is a relatively new state, so a home in 1955 is really old by comparison. Where I grew up in Wisconsin, a 1955 build is not all that old at all. In the east coast, some would consider it just outside of new construction.

When I'm doing my initial analysis, prior to driving the property, I put in a default number to see if I'm in the ball park with respect to the opening bid. What I'm going to outline next is not a formula, but the basis of  my default number prior to visually seeing the property and reworking my repair number from a visual inspection. I typically add $5000 for every decade as a default. So a home in the 1980s would have a $25,000 default repair number prior to me driving the property. Some of you may be wondering why I do that at all since I'm going to drive it anyway. There are times the opening bid price is high and by gauging my bid price prior to driving it, I often save myself a trip. If my max bid estimate prior to driving the property is $10,000 or $20,000 below the opening bid, I may not even take the time to drive it. That comes with experience, and there are times a house is in pristine condition and you can still buy it with enough spread. Early on, drive them all to ensure you don't miss out on a great deal.

Since 1998 I have successfully completed over 200 fix-and-flip properties for myself. Today, I can estimate repairs fairly easily because I know what things cost. It's the expensive items you need to get familiar with: AC and heating units, roof work, landscaping, and interior and exterior paint to name a few. When starting out, the best recommendation is to know the details of your subject property: year built, square footage, etc. Then call around to different suppliers for pricing. Over time you won't need to make the call because you'll inherently know the costs.

Next is "carrying costs". If you're using cash, this part is easy. If you are borrowing money you need to account for the cost of the loan throughout the term of the project. I like to use a 120 day rule when flipping properties. Meaning, if I buy it today, I need to price it such that I am out with my anticipated profit in 120 days or less. This also gives me three turns on my money in a year so making 10% on a turn equates to a 30% annual return, all other factors being equal. I always like to add one or two months' worth of hard money expense when doing my calculations because there are times the deal doesn't sell in the fastest timeframe. This is a critical step if you're starting out to ensure the highest possible profit. If you are not familiar with hard money, review the previous chapter on the benefits of leveraging hard money, how to find it, and using it to your advantage.

"Closing costs" are all those that don't fall under the cost of money or repairs. Items such as insurance, utilities, acquisition fees (if you utilize a third-party bidding service), realtor commissions when you list to sell, etc. Few auctions have additional costs outside the actual purchase price. Keep in mind that the auctions where we buy are considered "absolute" and the auctioneer and trustee are paid by the beneficiary. I don't do business with other auctions that impose upfront load fees to the purchase. I prefer to buy direct without extraneous fees, and this book is all about saving you time and money.

Now let's examine the "profit" factor. Without profit, there's no point in this, right? On the Max Bid Sheet, I use the acronym MAP which stands for "minimum acceptable profit". While everyone wants to maximize their profits, as do I, you need to play the game in a seemingly counterintuitive way and bid with the intent to make minimal acceptable profit. If you don't, you'll face getting outbid on a regular basis because your profit goals are set too high. I have talked to many investors over the years that tell me they don't play in this space because they can't make the profits they're looking for. I see it in a different light – a way that supports the essence of this book – "How to make extraordinary profits from ordinary auctions." It's not about hitting a home run every time, but creating a consistent and sustainable process that brings in extraordinary profits by mastering a particular niche in

the market. I have literally run into these same "home run" investors one or two years later and discovered they have purchased zero properties while I've acquired and sold 10, 15, or 20 properties in the same time frame. Perhaps I didn't make enormous profit from any single transaction, but my investing income remained solid and consistent over time. Extraordinary from the ordinary all day long!

Ok, the math is simple. Start with market value and subtract everything else including profit and you end up with your max bid. This is the most you can safely bid at auction and protect your profit potential. As you just read, the two most important factors are market value and repairs. Don't be shy about getting a professional's opinion for either or both.

Remember we said earlier that in some places there might only be one bidder for a property you're interested in and sometimes they've won with a $1 over minimum bid? Remember also that's it a mistake to assume that a buck over is always a good deal?

A lender's strategy is to place the opening bid high enough to cover the outstanding balance of the loan, plus all fees they've attached to it, such as legal fees, late fees, and the probable agent commission they will have to pay if they take back the property and sell it through MLS. They balance that against the headaches and effort they must expend if they are unsuccessful at selling it at the auction.

Here's the thing. Not everyone at the auction is an investor! There are sometimes people there who are just looking for a home to move into!

The person looking for a primary residence has a different motivation and price tolerance than an investor. That person may think $5,000 less than market value is a great deal, while the investor would never consider a property with that little spread between acquisition and eventual selling price.

So don't think that the opening bid is always going to be a deal for you.

So how do you do this analysis? Let's start by going over the items on the Max Bid Sheet. Most of this information is easy to get or figure out, other parts are more difficult, and some is plain guesswork. But the more educated your 'guess' is, the more accurate your analysis will be.

I'll tell you the truth here. My guesses are probably better than yours! Look, I don't claim to be the smartest guy in the world, but I've been around this business for 16 years and simply have a ton of experience. I can look at a property, know what year it was built, and estimate actual repair costs within a few hundred dollars. If you do this enough, you will get that good too! It was the Max Bid Sheet that helped me develop this level of accuracy, and I still use it today, even though I usually know beforehand what it's going to show.

If you don't have access to MLS, find a friend who's a realtor that can help you. There are websites, such as Zillow.com that give you their analysis of a particular property or neighborhood. With sites such as these, you can look at entire areas and see what similar properties are listed for and what recent sales were. Zillow gives you what they cleverly call a "Zestimate" of the value of every house in that neighborhood. It should be noted that information obtained from these sources are only ballpark numbers and should be treated as such. Zillow isn't the only online service for determining market value of a property. There are others that you can find on a simple request from Google or other search engine. However, when using anything other than MLS or what I outlined earlier about what FHA appraisers look for, you might get off track on this extremely important analysis factor.

The situation can a bit different in areas comprised primarily of 'one-offs'. These are neighborhoods where homes are of many different types and styles, all built by different builders, at different times. In areas like these, accurate comparables are difficult. Here a physical inspection of the property is a must and educated guesses are what you will rely on more than usual.

For the most part, the kinds of homes I look for are in neighborhoods developed by the same builder. There may be 4 or 5 different models, but they are all the same age and build quality. They also tend to be in that affordable zone, where most properties are at or near average market price.

Some investors who work with realtors ask them for a BPO, or Broker Price Opinion. Some pay a fee for this, which is normally around $200. However, many have agreements with their favorite realtor and in exchange for giving them the listings on any property they buy, the realtor stands ready to provide these important services at no charge to their investor clients.

In the next chapter we'll talk a lot more about 'driving a property', the process I use to do a physical inspection. As you will learn, sometimes you get to see the inside of the property and sometimes that's just not possible. Nonetheless I can always see the outside, know what year it was built, and make some assumptions about the inside!

As you see on the Max Bid Sheet, there is a breakdown of the areas you want to look closely at in order to estimate repair costs, and you'll notice that I ask you to add a "10% bump".

Here is the hard and fast rule of doing repairs. It always costs more and takes more time than you had planned! The 10% bump up is there to account for that. Trust me on this, you will need that extra 10% for actual repairs.

Some investors I work with have a "paint and carpet only" thought process when they approach bidding on a property at auction. That means if their inspection reveals it needs more than that, they aren't interested in that property. They know the exact costs of paint and new carpets and aren't interested in replacing appliances, plumbing, rewiring, etc.

In certain areas, (check with your local building department), any work that has anything to do with plumbing and electrical must be permitted and performed by a licensed person, and those costs can be high!

Paint and carpet, in almost all areas can be done by unlicensed workers and can be paid whatever you negotiate. If you end up doing this often, you will develop a "crew" of local painters and carpet layers who will do the work at below average prices to get the steady work. You'll have your reliable team of "guys".

It's a good idea to keep a file on all the different tradesmen. You will go through some you'll never want to see again before you settle on those who are reliable and do good work.

Creating the Bid

After we have a good estimate of all costs, we can begin to determine what our max bid will be. You must take into account the opening bid, which is most often

Working off a sound platform of data saves both time and money.

published beforehand and how much over that you are willing to go. That will be your maximum bid!

Is the maximum bid actually the price you will pay? Not necessarily! If you are the only bidder on a property, you may only have to pay $1 over the opening bid. This happens more often than you would think. Whenever I see the auction results and I see a property that sold for any number ending in 1, such as $150,001, I can tell there was only one bidder and he/she paid one dollar over the opening bid.

This is the reason I use the MAP method for profit as it makes me more effective at the game of bidding. When I have a max bid of $125,000 on a particular property and I ultimately win it for 109,500, I truly celebrate not just the win but the additional profit. If my original gain was going to be $12,000 on my max bid, winning it at $109,500 pumps my profit up to $27,500, an additional $15,500!

The entire scenario depends on many things, but the location and the size of the spread between acquisition

and probable selling price will determine the competition. If there's a big spread in a hot area, count on plenty of potential buyers being there ready to bid! If the spread is smaller, and in a less desirable area, you may be the only bidder.

Smaller counties with fewer players will result in increased profits. If you're asking yourself if this will work in my small county, the answer is yes! There may be fewer properties going to sale, but you will tend to meet less competition. Profits will be bigger so get out and play!

There will be differences in various parts of the country. In nicer areas of Florida and California, there will always be competition. In Detroit, Michigan, you might be able to bid less than $20,000 and be the only contender.

In Phoenix where I live, certain parts of the metropolitan area like Scottsdale, Paradise Valley, and Gilbert are highly desirable areas while other areas are....not as desirable. Always remember that what seems like a place you would not ever want to live may be like a castle to someone else.

The basic formula comes down to this:

Eventual selling price of the property **minus** all the costs of fixing **minus** the profit margin (the amount you take to the bank) = your maximum bid.

Important Concepts

1. Numbers are everything in this space.
2. Trust your numbers.
3. Use a simple tool like the max bid sheet to calculate and track your numbers.

Chapter 8

Driving the Property

"Never trust to general impressions, my boy, but concentrate yourself upon details."

Sir Arthur Conan Doyle, 'The Adventures of Sherlock Holmes'

For most investors that I know and work with, investing is a local activity. That is, they invest in a certain area they know and is relatively close to where they reside.

This makes sense, and it's easy to understand the reasoning behind it. If you know a neighborhood and the type of people who live in the area, there are fewer

Most investors prefer to buy and sell locally.

surprises to contend with. Investors don't like surprises! Some maintain a 20 minute rule: if they can't drive to it in 20 minutes, they're not interested.

Also locally, you are more likely to know about news that could affect resale and rentals in that area. Is a new elementary school planned within walking distance...or an adult bookstore and a liquor store?

That being said, I do work with investors from different states, and even foreign citizens who know and are interested in Arizona real estate. These people generally have a lot more money to invest, and wouldn't be in trouble if they lost money on one deal.

My assumption is that most people reading this book are local investors, people who intend to invest near where they live. This gives you the greatest opportunity to drive the properties beforehand to get an idea of the condition of the property, the type of neighborhood, the number of homes for sale in the area, and other criteria that you will use to decide to pursue the property.

First, a discussion on timing. In some areas like Arizona, homeowners that miss three payments (typically), are issued a "Notice of Default" at least 90 days before the scheduled sale. That's not when you want to drive the property. If I haven't said it before, buying at auction is something I do daily but more than that I look today at tomorrow's auctions and no further out. Again, it's looking today for tomorrow, every day. There is a constant stream of properties every day and jumping all around looking too far in advance would wear on me. If you want to be successful in this game, keep the window tight and enjoy the enormous profit potential.

During the 90 day default period, many things can happen that will affect whether that property will actually be auctioned. The homeowner may somehow get the money to reinstate the loan. The lender, usually a bank, might restructure the loan, or perhaps grant a loan modification. (Remember – the bank does not want to take back the house if there is any other plausible solution.) The homeowner declares bankruptcy – this usually does not mean the house will not be sold at auction, but during the period the debtor is under protection of the bankruptcy court, no action can be taken. In my experience, this just puts off foreclosure by a month or two. A mortgage or deed of trust where the home is collateral for the loan is not discharged in bankruptcy. There just can't be any legal action during that period of time. This period of time varies by state. In Arizona, it is 28 days for a normal bankruptcy, but make sure you know the laws of the state you are investing in!

The best time to drive a property you are interested in acquiring is after a minimum bid has been established which can be as little as three days before the auction scheduled date, so time is of the essence.

My rules for driving a property I am going to bid on are:

- Drive every property. (or I can't bid)
- Drive it the night before or the morning of the auction.
- Get as close a look as possible.
- Lock it up tight on my way out. (if I was able to get in)

I can't tell you the number of times I had a client "bid blind" on a property and be very unhappy with the result. My rule is if you couldn't get there, you can't bid. Period! I always drive the night before or the morning of to ensure the most current view of the property, reducing risk of damage, fire, etc. If it is occupied, I am always respectful to the current occupant, whether it is a tenant or the home owner. If it is the home owner, I know they have had a tough year and don't need me and 20 of my closest friends (competition) showing up and asking to come inside. I take a look and keep on going. If the home is vacant, I will always take the best look possible, including entering the property for the closest look. I never break and enter! Lastly, if I can get in, I always lock it up tight. Why? Two reasons. First, if I'm the successful bidder, I don't want anyone coming in after me and taking anything. Second, if my competition can't get in behind me, I have an edge at auction.

When I drive a property, I always want to get as much information on that property as possible. I park in front and first determine as best I can if the property is vacant or occupied. Many homes that are days away from being sold at auction are already vacant, but it's not the rule by any means.

One extra trick I have learned that gives me an edge when bidding, is to look up my subject property on MLS and see if there is a current or recent listing that can shed light on my potential project prior to heading out. Looking for things like occupancy, damage, length of time vacant, condition, etc. Often the listing has photos that show the property condition at one moment in time.

I can infer certain things if the house appears to have people living in it. If it is occupied, then the bathrooms probably work. In Arizona where summertime temperatures go as high as 120 degrees, air conditioning is not a luxury, it's a necessity of life. If it's summer, there is a good possibility that the air conditioning works.

What to Look For

If the property is occupied, I proceed with caution. I try to see all areas I can see from the street without actually going onto the property itself, and take photos.

If the property is unoccupied, there are many more options! I can go onto the property, examine closely the outside of the house, and begin my assessment of how much money I will need to spend on the exterior of the house if I were to acquire it. I look at the landscaping, the exterior paint condition, the roof, and anything else I can see. I often will look in the windows if I can to determine what shape the interior is in. I have seen everything from what appears to be a well maintained home to a house with missing drywall, copper pipes pulled out, carpets deeply stained and torn or even missing.

Everything you can learn about the property is important for determining your maximum bid.

The most important items I am interested in regarding the interior are the condition of the kitchen and bathrooms. I almost always do paint and carpet, so their condition is pretty much irrelevant. However, a heavily damaged kitchen in a home built in 2000 is a set back if I didn't plan for it.

If I am very sure the house is vacant, I try the front door to see if it is locked.

Before I continue, I need to make clear that in no way am I encouraging anyone to break and enter a home, even if it is vacant! Know the laws in your area. Even if a house is vacant, someone other than you owns it. Being inside the premises without permission may be trespassing or breaking and entering, both of which carry serious criminal charges.

Also, neighbors who see an unknown person entering the home may very well call the police. Telling them that you are an investor considering buying the place may not go over well and could result in spending a day in the local jail. It may come down to whether or not you have permission to be inside the house. If the answer is NO, then you could be charged. So to sum up.....Don't break the law!

However......if you can gain entrance through an *unlocked* door, you will learn a lot about the property and get a much better idea as to the costs for the necessary repairs. You can see and test the conditions of the bathrooms, the kitchen, the walls, light fixtures, etc.

There is nothing like gaining access to the interior of the house to give you the best information about its condition, and whether or not you should try to acquire the property.

As I've told you, I have purchased homes at auction that look like the family cleaned and vacuumed the house on their way out the door. In others, it appears they played demolition derby the night before their exit. Sometimes you just aren't going to know, but there are some clues. I have found that if the exterior of the house is well maintained, the inside will probably be too. Conversely, while not always the case, when the outside is trashed, the inside will be too.

If you're a fix-and-flip investor who wants only to invest in new carpets and paint, and perhaps some minor landscaping, then it's best to cross off your list any property whose exterior is in bad condition and access to the interior is not possible.

However, a property in bad condition is not necessarily a negative thing – depending! A property needing a lot of repair will most likely have fewer bidders, giving you the opportunity to acquire it for less. In the case of no sale, it reverts back to the lender, and will most likely be listed with a real estate agent within two to three months. A "Broker

Price Opinion" will be ordered by the bank and an asset management company will be hired to handle repairs and manage its sale. So, if you remain interested in the property, you'll still have the opportunity to make an offer on it through conventional means. Unlike at auction, where you cannot bid lower than the published opening bid, you can offer any amount you want.

Back to driving the property. It has often been said that knowledge is power. No more is this the case than in foreclosure investing. The more knowledge you have about the property, the more confident you can be about your bid and the greater probability you will be able to make money on the deal.

Still, what about the out of town bidder? A lot of foreclosed property is purchase by out-of-towners, sometimes people out of the country. How can they see what they are bidding on? Some don't care and are just playing the odds, and as I said, many of these people can afford to absorb some losses if they are buying a lot of properties or buying very frequently.

A few years ago, I partnered with a mobile videographer who produces 5 minute or less video reports on each property he is assigned. Sometimes I am too busy to drive across town to do a drive by of a very attractive property I am interested in. This service does a great job. I have instructed them carefully what the investor wants to see, and they accurately make a video report from an investor's perspective.

I am not the only one who offers this service. Right now my video team just does central Arizona, including Phoenix and vicinity. If you are investing in another part of the country, I'm sure you can find a similar service. The price is nominal, so if you're investing out of your area, it's worth every penny. These reports can be sent via email, any cloud storage service, or any other technology that sends videos online.

Important Concepts

1. Be respectful with occupied properties.
2. Drive every property you plan to bid on.
3. Be safe, don't take reckless chances when out driving properties.

Chapter 9

Presale Due Diligence

"The primary reason critical due diligence for real estate is so important is to ensure that the buyer knows exactly what he/she is purchasing… It should involve physical inspections of the real estate, an assessment of related-environmental conditions, a review of the title, zoning requirements, contracts, leases, and surveys. "

Marc, Entrepreneurial Insights

The following are the areas of due diligence you should be most concerned with:

- Property Location (legal description)
- Lien Position
- County taxes in arrears
- Judgments and assessments and HOA liens
- Federal and State Tax liens

One of the most overlooked pre-auction due diligence tasks is establishing the accurate property location. The

A property's location is not necessarily obvious.

determining source is the legal description. Most notices of default will use language similar to "purported address: 1234 N Fox Street", and will give a lengthy legal description. The legal description is the only true identifier of a parcel of real estate. While it happens rarely that there is a discrepancy, it can be an occasional heart breaker. In 16 years, I am aware of several bid wins at auction that were inaccurate. The new property owner came to find out she had actually purchased the house next to the one she really wanted. Again, even though it is a rare occurrence, I bring it up because it is so often overlooked and so important.

Lien position can be a very costly mistake if not taken seriously. My best advice is to create a relationship with a title company and plan on buying title insurance from them for the subject property. The basics follow this logic: when buying a first position lien, all junior liens drop off including federal and state tax liens. However, sometimes it is the second lien holder bringing the property to foreclosure. In that case, the first lien holder does not go away. If you mistakenly buy a second position lien, you're taking title to the property subject to the first. Buying second position liens intentionally can, in rare cases, be a profitable approach if handled

correctly, but is very much an advanced strategy. Again, you're subject to the first, so paying it off or modifying it is required to protect your ownership. I am often asked whether one can negotiate the note down with the first lien holder. From my experience, the answer is usually NO. A first position beneficiary will celebrate that someone stepped up to buy that position. They know that you will have to pay them off to secure the property and now they're in a stronger position.

Delinquent county taxes (property taxes) always pass to the new owner, even at auction. All county taxes are treated the same way for all auctions I am aware of. Whether the winning bidder at auction is a third party, like you or me, or the beneficiary taking it back, that next party is responsible. Most county assessors allow online access to the general public making it easy to research delinquent taxes. Regardless of any  delinquencies, you will always be liable for a prorated amount of current taxes owed, as with any traditional title conveyance. Most county taxes are assessed, billed and paid twice per year. The shrewd investor defers any taxes owed and takes care of them at close of escrow when the property is resold.

Talk about not knowing what you don't know... Back in 1999, I was on my third or fourth flip and was reviewing my settlement statement. Beside the normal proration of taxes due, there was an additional line item labeled "back taxes" of $400. I called the escrow officer and explained that this couldn't be mine – had to belong to the previous owner. Needless to say, she laughed out loud and I was embarrassed. That's the definition of an expensive lesson. While a $400 hit to my profit didn't sour my deal, it could have been a lot worse and from then on taxes in arrears was an item I researched and planned for carefully in all my future buys. Again, that lesson could have been a lot more expensive – I was lucky!

Regarding judgments, city assessments, and HOA liens, it really depends on your state laws. I highly recommend sitting down with your title partner and going over all these items that can affect your buy at auction. Knowing is half the battle. Let me give you a few examples. In Arizona, HOA liens get dropped through the auction process. Their only recourse is to go after excess proceeds, if there are any. In Nevada, HOA liens are considered a super lien and do not drop off. An HOA will also collect 9 months up front dues from the new owner at auction. This is not a reason to avoid Nevada, but simply something to be aware of and understood so you can safely capitalize on what is available in the market

 of auction buys. Take your title partner out to lunch or have a sit down with them and ask about the effect of the following in your buy at auction: city and county assessments, HOA liens, mechanics liens, child support liens, active law suits, etc. You get the idea.

Federal and state tax liens scared me more than anything until I understood the basics. They fall off in the auction process. For past due federal taxes, the IRS has the option of a 120 day redemption period within which they are allowed to place the lien back on the property. Having explained that little tidbit, no one, including myself or any title officer has ever seen the IRS take advantage of this post auction. With that in mind, title companies will not issue a policy insuring against an IRS lien for those first 120 days post sale. Or they'll issue a policy with the IRS appearing on schedule B (items excluded). Most title companies possess the ability to work with the IRS and remove the cloud in the 120 day period. Feel free to contact us at INFOclosure.com, 480-686-9945, and we can assist you in the process of removing the cloud on title. Keep in mind, this is not a relevant issue for buy-and-hold investors as it will drop off in 120 days anyway. For the aggressive fix-and-flip investors seeking to turn the property in 120 days, you will need an intervention from a title company or INFOclosure.com. As for state tax liens, you will need to check with your individual state's department of revenue.

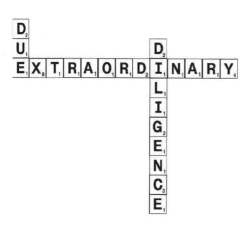

Driving the properties you are interested in is a very important part of the entire due diligence package which we discussed in the last chapter. There are many other areas that you must pay attention to also. Some of these things you can do yourself and for some you will need the help of other services like licensed real estate agents, title agencies, and sometimes a real estate attorney.

Remember this – the due diligence you perform will mitigate a lot of the risks associated with real estate investing. Doing it properly and thoroughly can mean the difference between making a nice profit or disaster!

Most investors are savvy about the numbers end of the foreclosure investment market. However, they lack the ability to perform proper due diligence on the properties that they are interested in buying. Due diligence is simply the process of determining the true value of the potential investment. Much of the information about a property is public record which you can uncover yourself if you have the time and the inclination.

I encourage investors I work with to use professionals for most of this, as they can often get information much quicker than you can. They may be privy to certain sources providing them with discovery in minutes as opposed to what would take hours by yourself.

Yes, there are nominal fees for this information, but time is money and I have always found that paying these fees is much less expensive than the cost of my time. If you begin investing in foreclosed real estate full time, there will never be enough hours in a day for you to perform all necessary research.

One of the first and most important necessities is  engaging a title company to perform a title search on a property, so as to uncover any liens against it. Some liens fall away after the deed is transferred, and some do not. Again, the primary example being county taxes, as I have previously discussed. There is no way to know this without a title search. Any liens against the property will not be known or disclosed by the Trustee at the auction. So if there is a large property tax lien and you acquire that property, that amount is now your debt!

Fortunately, most property taxes in arrears are not that large, but you must know about them to figure your true cost of the property. In western states, property tax liability is usually low, in contrast to eastern states with very high property tax rates like New Jersey. A year's tax bill on an average home in Arizona is around $1,500. In New Jersey it may be $10,000 or more.

Mechanics liens are very common. A mechanics lien may be placed on a property for any work that may have been done by a contractor and was not paid for. These liens, in most states, last for 6 months only, and then fall away.

Other common liens you should look for:

- Easements
- Judgments
- 2nd Mortgages

Not all, or any of these may be your responsibility if you

acquire the property. Check with a local real estate attorney if you find any of these liens to determine your potential liability for them.

Another part of due diligence is to research the properties in the surrounding area. The sale price of real estate is public record, so you should find out easily what properties in the surround area are selling for.

Sometimes, especially when time is of the essence, I use a local real estate broker to do a Broker Price Opinion, or BPO. There is usually a fee associated with this, but it is usually nominal, less than $100.

It would be well to repeat again that just because a property is going to foreclosure doesn't mean it's always a good deal! I have seen some opening bids that were well above what homes were going for in that area. No one is going to apologize or refund your money if you pay too much. This is raw, naked, capitalism, so you must protect yourself by knowing as much about the property as possible before bidding. Knowledge is power in the foreclosure game.

The title report will also show if there is any record of environmental contamination, another important piece

 of information that will help you determine the true value of that property. I look at the entire due diligence process as an elimination process. When I'm interested in acquiring a property for sale at the auction, and while I'm gathering information about it, I am concurrently looking for reasons to eliminate it from consideration. There is really no emotion in this process. It's all about the numbers and whether I can make a profit. I'm not going to live there!

Having completed researching the paper trail on your property, you are now ready to take a close look at the physical property itself. This is the part of due diligence that investors are either very good at, or miss

completely. There are many subtle features of a house that can make a big difference in its resale value on the open market. Inspecting for structural roof damage involves much more than just looking up at the roof and identifying a few shingles that need to be replaced. Either you, or the inspector that you hire, needs to get up onto the roof and look for any soft spots. You also need to get into the attic and inspect the roof deck from the underside. If you see areas where water has run down the rafters, then you'll need to be very certain that there isn't dry rot somewhere on the deck. This can be costly to repair and can take a big bite out of your re-sale profits. If you suspect there is dry rot, then you should also have the house checked for mold contaminations before you bid. If you're hoping to buy a foreclosure and turn it around quickly, then you should probably stay away from homes with any obvious structural problems. Again, take the time to perform the proper due diligence to avoid getting stuck with costly repairs.

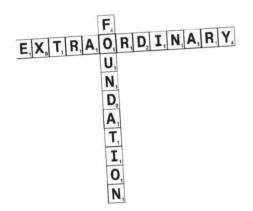

Look closely, if you can, at the foundation of a home. Sinking or cracked foundations require careful inspection to determine how severe a problem they are. Sometimes a crack is just a crack while other times it can be a signal that a house is ready to fall. Foundation repairs can be very costly and if you don't account for them in your investment plan they can chew up not only your profit but also the principle amount of your investment. In other words, make sure you go down into the basement, no matter how dark and dank, and carefully check the foundation.

Of course, if the property is still occupied, you won't be able to perform any of these inspections and will need to rely on your best educated guess. After a while, you can get very good at this. For me, after 3000 plus successful bids at auction on behalf of my clients, and another 250 for myself, I can pretty much create estimates hitting the nail directly on the head.

If you are not knowledgeable about home conditions or prices for typical repairs, it would probably be best having someone else you trust do these inspections for you. Some items cost more than you would expect, and in certain areas, you may have to use licensed contractors for certain work. You may also be required to get permits from the city for certain jobs and there are building code regulations that may need to come into account. Some jurisdictions have local laws that state if any structural work is being done, then the house must comply fully with updated codes, which can add a substantial amount to the repair bill.

Important Concepts

1. Research lien laws in your state to ensure safe buying practices.
2. Only bid on first position liens.
3. County taxes in arrears carry over to the buyer at auction.

Chapter 10

The Psychology of Bidding

"If you discovered something that made you tighten inside, you had better try to learn more about it."

Nicholas Sparks, Message in a Bottle"

The psychology of auctions is absolutely fascinating and it's something that all bidders should be aware of before auction day. Observing and understanding the often subconscious, psychological factors that influence

Learning the psychology has allowed me to get the best deals.

bidding is part of my business and helps me to get the best deals at auctions for my clients. When I succeed at that, they come back to me again and again.

If I had to pick a favorite chapter from this book, hands down it would be this one. There is a discernable mental procedure underlying this bidding process which I have identified after all these years and will outline for you as this chapter unfolds. Understanding the psychology of bidding and being able to apply its' principles is truly a doubled-edged sword. If your competition has a higher maximum bid in mind while you stay true to your number, you will lose no matter what you do. On the flip side, if you're bidding close to your competition, you can employ the techniques I'm about to outline and maintain a marketable edge. There is an old saying in poker: "If you haven't identified the amateur in the first five minutes, it's YOU!" Having personally bid on over 20,000 live property auctions, I have a little experience.

Any auction moment can become a highly emotional environment where a bidder's focus, reason, and common sense are easily lost costing them thousands! I have seen it happen countless times. In one of my previous chapters, I talked about the difference between extroverts and introverts. You need to take a close and honest look inside this important area, identify yourself as one or the other, and plan accordingly. I don't place a lot of importance on labels, but if one such label could cost me or make me

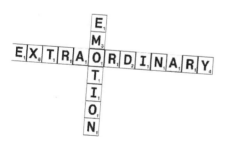

thousands of dollars in a real estate deal, I have no problem studying the subject and giving myself a little common sense edge.

As I said earlier, I am an "introvert" and in most situations am non-emotional and let numbers drive my investment decision to the exclusion of everything else. I have friends who could never play in the auction space because they're "extroverts" and emotionally driven. Losing a deal there creates a storm of commotion and conversation that should never exist in this area. I show up and leave with the same game face. In fact, I celebrate the ones I don't win as much as those I do. If I didn't win a property, it was one I shouldn't have anyway. Whatever the outcome, my though process is masked behind my game face. I am very happy when I know I'm going to profit from a deal and create a very nice home for someone else to live in. What is just as satisfying is the fact that I didn't pay a dollar more than I said I would for other properties.

We talked about MAP (minimum acceptable profit) in the chapter on analyzing a deal. When I truly work toward my MAP, I never have any regrets about those I don't win. The numbers drive the buy, not emotion. I can't tell you how many times I've witnessed an emotionally charged amateur completely show their hand to the competition and pay far more than they had planned. I share that because I don't want it to be you. If you over pay for a $15 item on eBay, no big deal. That's not going to ruin you financially. Over paying for a property at auction could put some investors out of the game. Be patient, bid smartly, and celebrate the losses as much as the wins.

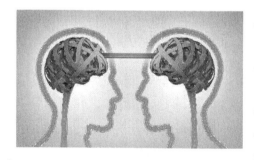

Just think about it. A group of people all want the same thing and in order to get it, they need to outbid and/or outsmart each other. Auctions are very much about competition and being a winner while trying to spend as little as possible – two elements that are in conflict with one other! To see this in action, go to a foreclosure auction in any larger city. You'll see folks franticly talking on their cell phones with investor giving them real time bidding positions on particular properties. Others are gathered around the Trustee's table waiting to see if their bid is the highest before the gavel drops, ready to counter any higher bid that may come up as time slips away.

This doesn't happen at every auction on every property. Here again, there is often only one bidder for a particular property and sometimes no one is interested. This happens when either the property is in bad physical condition, in a bad area, the title is so clouded that re-sale would be next to impossible, or for any other valid reason. There are also times when the competition just didn't take the opportunity to look at a deal and you

walk away a big winner. If you want to make extraordinary profits at ordinary auctions, you need to make sure you are playing full-out on every deal that meets your model. I play every day which allows me to capitalize on deals that others let fall off their radar. Again, if you want those extraordinary profits, play full-out! This is a fact. The lower the opening bid on established residential housing, the more competition there will be. Remember, for the fix-and-flip investor, the spread between the price you can acquire a property for and the price you can sell it for is the key ingredient for making a profit.

When one of those properties is for sale, expect that many interested buyers will be present with various bids in mind and don't for a second believe that the opening bid will be the price the house sells for! I've seen hundreds of auctions where an opening bid is, as an example $100,000 and the final win price was $145,000 or more. Everybody wants to win at a low opening bid level and many will drop out early in the bidding process as it becomes apparent that the actual selling price is going to be significantly higher.

So who or what determines an opening bid? The bank or the note holder does. They usually set that opening bid at what they are owed plus any and all fees that they can place on top of that! Attorney's fees, holding costs, late fees, document fees, FedEx fees, fax fees....just about any fee they can legally add on, they will.

So if the default amount of a loan is $100,000 and the fees the bank has imposed are $10,000, the opening bid will be $110,000, no matter what the actual value is. This is known as a credit bid. Very often you will see a property at auction with an opening bid of $110,000 and the actual market value is over $200,000. Imagine that, some people think. I can get a $200K house for $110,000! They are already spending the profits in their head!

$110K is of course not going to be the final win price, unless the house is in horrible condition or burned out. If it's a nice home in a good area, it's more likely going to be sold for a higher price.

Remember, there are people with very different motivations at auction, and each one has a different maximum amount they will bid based on their business model. A person who is looking for a good deal on a property they plan on living in as their primary home may be satisfied with getting the property for only slightly less than market value, while the fix-and-flip investor is out of the game when the spread between acquisition price and selling price is too slim to make a profit. The buy-and-hold investor is not going to be as sensitive on acquisition price; they plan to rent the property for monthly income and sell at a later date when the miracle of appreciation does its work.

Different motivations = different maximum bids!

So if there happens to be a lot of bidders on any given day seeking a home to be their primary residence, the fix-and-flipper is out of the bidding quickly. The worst thing for that kind of investor is to keep bidding when the possibility of a profit starts to evaporate.

Never forget that ensuring extraordinary profits at auction requires being in the space regularly. When you play at this level, you'll see many people come and go. Those who plan on living in a house and can pay cash will usually pay a higher amount because they can. Once they buy, you won't see them again. You'll experience novice investors as well as those that have been there seemingly forever. The experienced individuals typically get irritated with rookie players as they demonstrate their lack of knowledge and skill. Quite often the regulars will make every effort to take advantage of their inexperience. You should be aware that novices who show up to auction trying to make sense of the chaos are great candidates for doing business with. I created an entire business model just from meeting people at auction and sharing the information I put together. I can honestly say I made extraordinary profits from these ordinary auctions.

The key is discipline. Truthfully, if a property won't give me a $15,000 profit or thereabouts, I'm not very excited or interested. Yes, $10,000 is a nice profit, but for me it needs more potential than that to justify spending the time and incurring the additional risks that go along with investing in real estate. That, however, is just me. You will establish your own minimums based on your financial model and personal needs.

Have I ever bought a property and made less than $10K? You bet, but many of them made $25K profit and more. Those that netted me a lesser amount had unforeseen repairs requiring me to throw more cash into them than initially planned.

It's up to you to set your minimum profit potential when you start bidding at the foreclosure auction. Too low and you will work hard for little reward. Too high and you will have very few properties to bid on. I urge you to attend as many auctions as you can before you start actually bidding. You'll get to know what's going on and learn who the pros and the amateurs are.

Before I dive into the execution of the bid, I want to frame a couple of things regarding the psychology of bidding. In addition to showing up and observing often prior to actually bidding, my physical location when bidding is an important aspect. I need to be in close proximity to the auctioneer while maintaining a visual of my competition. I also like to position myself so I see new people showing up and can start a relationship and begin bidding for them. (Extraordinary profits mean capitalizing on every opportunity to serve the market.)

My placement in relation to the auctioneer is critical so that I don't miss them crying out a sale or missing a bid. At the same time, I like to keep my competition in sight and observe them closely as they're bidding. Almost all of them are on the phone with a client or business partner and they're constantly communicating sale activity back and forth. When they get close to their number, they naturally start to fidget and their body language changes dramatically. Looking harder and more intently into their papers is a common give away. Pacing faster and faster and/or ending their phone call clearly says they're getting close. The longer you play in this space the better you will get at noticing the competition's "give-aways". Have fun with it, but more importantly, be aware of how you show up and don't make the same costly mistakes.

Execution of the Bid

Executing the bid seems pretty straightforward, right? You present a higher bid than the other bidders, and this repeats until only you are left. You get the property! While this is true, my extensive experience of attending auctions has given me some insights about different ways to approach bidding, and some similar patterns you are likely to see.

Again, there are all kinds of people attending the auction, with many different strategies and business models and they bid differently, but these are the kinds of things you are likely to see.

The Grind

The Grind is the most common way bidding is done at auction. It's slower, and keeps lots of people involved until the price starts to go too high. In the Grind, someone offers $1.00 over the opening bid, and I follow up with "plus $100". It is irrelevant to me who opens the bidding at "plus a buck". I choose the Grind most often, as it makes it difficult for the competition to gauge where I am going when I'm in the monotone zone of "plus $100". This can go on for quite a while, which is why I call it the "Grind".

So very slowly, bidders start leaving the game. It can take a half hour or longer if that's the way it is going! If I suspect the actual winning bid will be around $150K, and the bidding is at $125K and each new bid increment is only $100, you can see it's going to take a while.

This is where it can get tricky and your emotions can come into play. When the bidding gets close to your 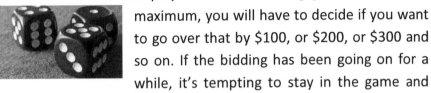 maximum, you will have to decide if you want to go over that by $100, or $200, or $300 and so on. If the bidding has been going on for a while, it's tempting to stay in the game and your competitive juices start to flow. YOU WANT TO WIN!

Now I know some investors with great discipline, who, when they reach their maximum, simply drop out if it goes higher, even by only $100. Others will go up a thousand or two from their previously determined maximum.

There is no right way or wrong way to do this. It's up to each bidder to know their hard limit.

I realize that it's hard to celebrate your losing bids as much as your winning bids, but that's what experienced investors learn to do. The temporary euphoria of the win can be replaced by the feeling that you paid too much and won't achieve anywhere near your profit model you had planned.

The second strategy is more abrupt. It's called...

The Shock

I have personally used the shock effectively and it goes like this. The opening bid is $100,000 and my competition is getting psyched up for the grind. I immediately jump the bid in $10,000 increments which is something they aren't expecting. While they are furiously trying to figure out my aggressiveness on this property I'm already one or two $10,000 bids in. This can cause them to stop and try to figure it out, thinking I'm running this property up. It has worked for me when they stop bidding out of confusion and I end up with the property

cheaper than if I had employed the Grind method. It doesn't work every time but it's so great when it does. It's a classic poker move. At the poker table there is often at least one "shock" player; someone who bids a LOT higher than the way the game is going. This scares away the people who probably shouldn't be there anyway.

This ends bidding from those who thought they were going to get the property for a steal, and they quickly move. This leaves the more 'serious' investors to play the game until one wins. After a shock bid, it can go right back into the Grind for the remaining investors!

In the beginning of my investing career, I did the Grind along with many other hopefuls. Today, I go more toward the shock route, so I quickly determine who the real competition is. Since I know a lot of serious investors, I have a sense of what kind of investor they are, what exit strategies they usually employ, and how much over their predetermined maximum they will go. Many know me or have heard of me and my team and that I have been doing this for years and sometimes the intimidation factor works in my favor.

Today, my team of bidders are often at auction bidding on behalf of my clients. They have them on the phone constantly updating them on the newest bid. My team knows the investors maximum, but because of this real time contact, the client can determine if he wants to go over the maximum and by how much.

When you go to the auction, those glued to their cell phones are usually bidding for others and know the game very well. You can learn a lot by watching them.

Important Concepts

1. Create a game face.
2. Bid with intellect, not emotion.
3. Celebrate the wins, celebrate the "did not win".

Chapter 11

Post Sale Due Diligence

"The expectations of life depend upon diligence; the mechanic that would perfect his work must first sharpen his tools."

Confucius

In a previous chapter we discussed the importance of pre-sale due diligence. Just as important, now that you own the property, are a series of things you must do after the fact to protect your investment.

The first critical post-sale task is insuring the property.

Here is your check list for post auction due diligence:

- Insurance
- Secure the property
- Eviction if needed
- Turn on utilities
- Home Inspection
- Remodel process

Of all the items you must do – and do right away – getting the property insured is tantamount to all others. The first phone call I make following every purchase at auction is to my insurance agent. I order so many policies that my agent and I are good friends today. I can't stress enough the importance of getting insurance on the asset immediately. If you're just starting out, you may need to educate your agent on exactly what you need. I buy a policy that is referred to as either a "builders risk" or "vacant home" policy. Don't let your agent tell you a "second home policy" or "landlord policy" will work for you. If you're remodeling for a flip

or prior to putting a renter in place, you need to have the correct policy. If something happens to the unit and the wrong policy is in place, even if your agent recommended it, there could be catastrophic results, especially in the event of a fire. I've had two fires and fortunately I was covered properly. Typically, the insurance company will try to deny the claim. Don't let that happen to you. Your insurance salesperson or broker is going to be one of your close associates on every purchase. The best insurance agents to know are the ones who work with investors and know the game

How do you find one? Ask a hard money lender, ask another investor – start with your current agent who takes care of your home and auto. While most real estate investors play their cards very closely, they'll give you the name and number of the insurance people they use. To them it's simply the person who they buy policies from. There are no trade secrets about this. I talk to the agent I buy most of my policies from well before any property is acquired. One quick call after the buy at the auction is done, and I have a policy on the property.

I really can't stress how important this is, and I just shake my head in wonder at some investors I know who don't make this their first priority. Just as in any other investment, your job is to remove as much risk as possible. The minute you own that property, anything that happens to it is your responsibility and will affect your bottom line. If the house burns down overnight, and you have no policy in place, you're out of luck and may have lost your entire investment. If someone falls on your property and makes a claim, it's your responsibility from the moment you own it.

Here in Phoenix where I do most of my investing, there are not a lot of weather related issues. We don't have earthquakes, there is virtually no flooding (it's the desert, after all), tornados and hurricanes don't affect us, and the weather is generally very mild. We can have severe dust storms. Despite very favorable conditions, the very first thing I do after acquiring a property is place homeowners insurance. You should too.

If you are a fix-and-flip investor and plan to be in and out of a property within a few months, an experienced

 insurance agent will tailor a policy to fit your situation, especially the ones who deal routinely with real estate investors. Find a good one and make her part of your "acquisition team".

The next phase in my post auction due diligence is securing the property. If the home is occupied, read my section on evictions later in this chapter. About 50% of the properties I buy are vacant and that has many

advantages. When vacant, getting in is generally not an issue. That aside, make sure you have a reliable lock smith as part of your team.

Here's another of my favorite and best trade secrets. I key every property to the same key. I call it a "common key". It's not a master key, but years ago I picked one key and always had the locks changed to use the common key. When I have the locksmith come out, they rekey everything to my common key. Everything!

I got the idea for a common key early on when I was trying to unlock a door of one of my projects and had to go through a huge multitude of keys. I was so frustrated  with standing there in 110 degree heat that the idea of keying everything the same became beyond obvious. Using a common key has other benefits. Over time, as I developed relationships with various tradesmen, I would give them a common key and let them know it would open all my properties. My flooring, HVAC, plumbing, cabinet, and handymen all had my key. The convenience of all my service providers having the same key is invaluable. Remember, time is money. No longer did I have to drive 45 minutes to a project, open a door and wait 10 minutes for the flooring to be measured, to then drive 45 minutes home. Common key = common sense!

The goal in securing the property is to ensure no one enters that you don't want in there. Don't forget windows, sliding glass doors, and garage doors. Just recently, I had a garage door that wasn't properly secured, and lost my new appliances that were installed as we finished up the remodel. That was a $1600 mistake.

The next step is turning on all utilities. Sometimes turning on utilities can be a hassle as the previous owner has an unpaid balance and you may be required to pay a large security deposit prior to turning anything on. The individual assisting you might ask for a settlement statement or a lease to turn on utilities. You will have neither when buying from auction. You will have a copy of the receipt for a property paid. Keep in mind the deed won't get to you for a week or two, but you don't want to wait that long. I became frustrated every time I set up utilities on a new project and it got worse as I increased my volume. I finally went down and talked to a manager and got a letter on file allowing me to set up 10 properties at one time with no deposit required. Again, time is money.

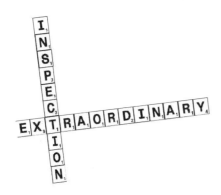

The next thing I do is order an inspection from a licensed home inspector – you'll see why in a moment. As a beginning fix-and-flip investor, my deals often ran into a snag in the 11th hour. It is common practice for the buyer of your newly redone investment to order an inspection and they should. In certain instances however, a buyer will waive their right to inspect for a variety of reasons, not the least of which is the almost negligible cost. Try not to allow this and if they insist, have them sign a disclaimer. You have a higher chance of ending up in court when they don't get their own home inspection.

After an inspection is done, the buyer's agent sends over a "buyer inspection and sellers response" document. This is the document that puts the seller on notice for items the buyer finds unacceptable and wishes to have repaired. I have four options at this point: fix everything, fix nothing (and risk losing the deal), fix only certain items, or offer a financial credit in lieu of repairs. Lenders, especially VA, often have items they require be repaired prior to closing.

I never want someone to get buyer's remorse and back out of a deal. Buyer's remorse many times starts with the home inspection and home inspector. Most investors put "lipstick on a pig" and call themselves pro-investors. I call them amateurs. The pro's get an inspection before and remodel accordingly. The most important thing to keep in mind is that the buyer and his agent often show up toward the end of the home inspection, and this is where the trouble can begin. The buyer enthusiastically asks, "How does it look?" Inspectors normally can't hide their body language or modify their verbiage, so if they have found issues, they say so. The buyer has immediate doubts and your deal is at risk!

When it is inspection time on my flips, the conversation goes in a different direction. Keep in mind, I start my projects with a home inspection of my own, hand the report to my project foreman, and give instructions to fix the items on the list. Now a new buyer comes in with their inspector and the conversation takes on a much more positive tone. Buyer asks, "How does it look?" Inspectors says, "It looks good. I found a couple of minor things, but overall it looks really good." Deal saved!!! This is going to cost you anywhere from $100 to $400 depending on your location, but it is money well spent.

After doing this for many years, I can walk into a property and, based upon its age and condition, make a pretty fair estimate of what the fixing project is going to cost, but I still get it done every time.

If you are a novice at this, the inspection report will be

a very important document! It will tell you what needs to be fixed, and serves as a roadmap for the project. The inspector will know the local laws and building codes that are important to figuring out how much it will all cost. Some cities will require you to pull permits, and may have codes that need to be observed, all of which can add considerable expense to the project. I try to get this done on homes BEFORE I buy them, but it is most often impossible on homes purchased at public auction.

Yet another task to take care of almost immediately after becoming the new owner of the property is to get title insurance. I get my title company involved during the pre-sale due diligence to determine if there are any liens on the property or second mortgages, tax bills, etc. I didn't add this to the post sale due diligence because it was previously ordered, but now that I own the property I need to pay for it to get the coverage I am looking for. I have the title insurance done early on. Some novice investors ask me why, and this is what I tell them: If you don't have title insurance, a claim of ownership of the property can come out of nowhere. A cousin of the former owner may come forth and claim that his cousin said he could have the house or that he gave him a share of the ownership. These are generally nuisance claims, but they can hold up the sale of the property after you have done your fix up and are ready to sell. Title insurance policies take care of any issues like this that come up.

I've recommend several things that will cost you money and make your profit a bit smaller, but serve to protect your precious investment. Remember this mantra: As a real estate investor, your biggest job is to moderate and eliminate as much risk as possible!

Some other things I do in terms of due diligence after the sale:

- I change the locks on the house. Every time. You don't know how many people have keys to this house. Probably the entire family of the previous owner, and anyone else they decided to give keys to.

This does not usually involve whole new locksets. Most homes today have one of three brands of locksets on their house. A locksmith can remove the cylinder and just rearrange the pins to your common key of choice so that all keys that are out there will no longer work. On some higher end and/or older homes, this may not be the case and the old hardware may have to be replaced. Some house locksets are key restricted, meaning the blanks are not readily available and may require more expense. Almost all average homes have Quickset, Schlage, or other massed produced locksets that are easy and inexpensive to change. Make sure you get enough keys for you, the real estate agent lock box, and the general contractor for the repairs.

- I also line up a real estate agent who will handle the sale. For me, that's not a problem as I own a real estate brokerage, but most of the investors I work with use an agent who is familiar with real estate investors and how they do business. Unfortunately, there aren't a lot of them around! This is where your connection with other investors will help. Many investors I work with, especially the ones who buy multiple properties every year, work with one or two agents who understand the fix-and-flip game, and in most cases don't get the regular real estate agent commission. Some investors pay them a flat rate per property, or a range of commission depending upon certain factors.

I recommend using agents for the sale. Again, some of my investor friends sell their properties privately to maximize every dollar of profit, but agents can do two very important things for you. One, they get a property into the multiple listing service, and two, they can handle getting an official BPO or broker price opinion done for you.

Unless you have another way to market your property when it's ready to sell, the MLS system is how your property is going to be seen by other agents, and only licensed real estate agents and  brokers have access to this system. I have never sold a house "by owner" or from a sign in the front yard. Every deal was sold by an agent finding my property on MLS and bringing their client by and subsequently presenting an offer. Believe me, I wanted to save the 4% to 6% fee just like you, but I learned that MLS brought buyers quicker than any other approach. As I mentioned early in the book, I got my license so I could list my own properties and did save some money, but I still offer 3% to the buyer broker to bring deals to me. It's well worth it, as it allows me to turn my money faster and that is the name of the game.

You may be starting to wonder if there is any room for profit after all this post-sale due diligence. The key is that I plan all these expenses during the pre-sale process. They are part of the numbers I put into the equation when determining my maximum bid. If the deal doesn't work with all these expenses in it, I pass on that deal and move on to one of many others.

If you take away anything from this chapter, and indeed this book, it's that smart, successful real estate investors always seek to mitigate and eliminate risk from their investment activities.

I don't want to end this chapter without talking about evictions. Back in 1998, I started buying at auction and had the list of everyone being foreclosed on, so I started to work pre-foreclosures. I would contact the home owner and work out a deal where I would purchase their home and they would move onto their next adventure. I could write an entire book on the subject, but can sum it up with a few sentences for you. Needless to say, I moved all my focus back to auction buying for these reasons. Working with distressed home owners is a lot of work, is very taxing, and is not for everyone. The time it takes to close the home is much longer than the auction, typically 45 days, and if a short sale is involved it will take much longer, if it ever happens at all. Working with home owners is emotionally taxing – that is if you have any ethics or morals. Many investors don't.

There are two ways to approach an eviction. You hire a law firm to evict the home owner or perform the eviction yourself. The eviction process is the worst part of buying at auction. The reality is that it has to be done to protect your asset and get the profit you are due with respect to the purchase. I have personally taken on sixty-five evictions out of the 200 or so flips I have done. Success or failure comes down to one thing and that is how you show up. It takes empathy and understanding to deal with hold over tenants (the previous home owners). This is the worst part of working auction properties, but is something that must be handled.

In my experience, I always try to do the eviction myself. I have been successful in getting the desired result — them out and me starting my project. The fact is they know they have to go, but rarely do they plan for it. The following is an outline of my approach to getting them out.

Firstly, I look at the tax records so I know who I am going to be asking for at the door. I know they are expecting me, but don't really want me to show. I drive up and park out front on the street. I knock on the door and ask, "Are you Mr. Smith?" Once I know I am talking to the right person I ask my next question: "I represent Flipping Homes, LLC, the company that bought your home at auction. Are you aware it went to auction today?" Regardless of the answer, I roll right into my next question: "Have you made any plans for moving out?" Typically the answer is no, and while all this conversation is going on I am assessing everything I can about the property: damage, moving boxes, dogs, etc. If you follow my script, so far I am asking questions to keep them engaged. My next question is: "The Company has authorized me to give you $500 in exchange for keys if you can be out in 5 days. Would $500 help you out?" I could keep going on but I think you get the picture. My goal is to take over the property with little to no damage and I want to keep the fixtures in place. Often the homeowner says something like they  just put the range in and are taking it, or the light above the table is a family heirloom. I will want to discuss the range but will not argue the family heirloom. You have to choose your battles. One of my keys to success in evictions is I say, "The company has also authorized me to say you don't need to clean up or haul unwanted stuff away." It's amazing how powerful this statement is. You literally see their shoulders drop in relief. Can you imagine having to move your entire house and family in 5 days? Me neither! Giving them the opportunity to take their "stuff" and leave is a benefit to all parties. I typically get people out quicker and I don't care if the house is not cleaned or has personal items that need to be removed. A couple of guys and a dumpster makes fast work of it and gets my project underway quicker. I have negotiated for a few extra dollars and a little extra time on a few occasions but typically hold to my $500 in 5 days. Remember, it's all in how you show up. Show up looking for a fight and you will get just that. Show up with empathy and understanding and you'll enjoy a mutually beneficial result.

The biggest mistake new fix-and-flip investors make is to "sympathize" and not "empathize" with the occupant and try to make them a tenant. Worst decision ever! First off, you need to get them out and stay true to your exit strategy. Second, they didn't pay the mortgage, why would they pay you rent?

Your second option is to hire an attorney whose practice it is to do evictions. I use one of the big firms in town that has done over 100,000 evictions. These guys know their stuff and because of the volume, their price is very affordable. It typically takes three weeks to get them out and ends with the Constable knocking at the door. I always prefer to do it myself. 90% of the time I have them out in less than three weeks and put out $500 which is close to what we pay for an attorney to go through the "forcible detainer action".

Here in Arizona, when you get the call from the Constable you agree on a time to meet at the property. You have to be there and he tells you to bring a locksmith. When the Constable knocks on the door with his night stick there is no mistaking that someone of authority has arrived. The second the door is open the Constable puts his foot in so the door cannot be shut again. The home owner requests more time, the

Constable looks over at you, your response is no and he relays the message and calls the locksmith over. The family is literally put out on the street right there. The doors are rekeyed and windows secured and then you set up a time for the homeowners to come back and take their belongings if they don't pull them out right then. I don't like to see this done in the fashion described above. I much prefer to negotiate the homeowners exit in a peaceful fashion. Keep in mind also that you cannot physically force anyone out of a home. Only the Constable, on court order, can do that.

Always consult an experienced attorney to support your evictions.

Important Concepts

1. Get proper insurance on the asset immediately.
2. Approach evictions with respect.
3. Time is of the essence.

Chapter 12

Wrapping It Up

"Nothing can stop the man with the right mental attitude from achieving his goal. Nothing on earth can help the man with the wrong mental attitude."

Thomas Jefferson

In the preceding 11 chapters of this book, I believe I've shared with you all the aspects of how I invest in real estate and have made a fortune doing so. I hope that I have given you a blueprint with which you can duplicate my success or perhaps your version of success in buying foreclosed properties at the auctions that happen all over this country every business day.

A blueprint for success.

I also hope that after reading this book, you don't just put it on a bookshelf somewhere and forget about it. That was never my intention.

Two things are important to me: life style and legacy. Investing in real estate and specifically buying at public auction has allowed me to create a life style beyond what I ever thought possible. Lifestyle is more than money, but don't get me wrong, money is important. Having freedom with my time helps me define what a great life style is. While I choose to spend a lot of time at the office, I get to dictate my personal time as well and that is what a great life style is all about. Having control of your time and your health is invaluable and the money is just a bonus!

I left corporate America back in 1998, and never looked back. That was a great time in my life. I learned a lot and met and worked with some incredible people. You don't have to stop what you are doing and invest in real estate full time to improve your lifestyle – that just happened to be my path. Many people begin buying real estate while they work full time. What I opened up to you in the preceding chapters is my primary acquisition strategy allowing me to buy at the lowest price point in the market and in the shortest time. If buying at auction were simple, I would not have written this book. It's not. There are risks, but with those risks come the rewards we are all after. The "dots" connect in traditional real estate. If you want to buy a home in the traditional way, find an agent and the process unfolds almost seamlessly.

The process of writing this book is part of what I call my legacy. I know the importance of contribution – it's a fundamental human need we all have. I spent the last 16 years buying in a space that has natural barriers to entry, and once you get in you're not met with people who are glad to see you! The fact remains however, there are extraordinary profits to be made. This book was set up to show that not only is it a viable acquisition strategy, but also provides a process to capitalize on it. It is my desire that my work, books, educational platforms, and companies serve people long after I am gone. That will be my legacy.

It's a little known secret in the "how to" books and seminar world, that very few people ever take the action necessary to do what they wanted to learn about! The bold truth is that of all the thousands – TENS of thousands – of people who attend real estate investment seminars, fewer than 5% ever do anything with the training; they never buy an investment property!

This, to me, is sad. I firmly believe that real estate investment is the one thing the average person can do to achieve wealth in their lifetime. It's very financially rewarding, but like every other worthwhile activity, you have to know and understand all the risks, follow a plan, and follow through.

It's not a "get rich quick" scheme. Almost all if not all get rich quick schemes out there are scams. The only people who get rich quick are the people who start it. Everyone else gets fleeced. I think this is common knowledge among most people, but there are still so many who fall for the promises and part with their hard earned money, with no return – ever.

Please don't be one of those people who do nothing with the knowledge and tips you've learned in this book.

In the beginning, it's okay to be scared! I was! Nonetheless, if you stick to the guidelines I discussed in this book, you will make money and will become more confident with each successive deal you are involved with.

Some people like to take a partner on their first deals; someone who has been successful before. That's a great strategy. Where do you find other investors who will do deals with you? Every city I know of has real estate investment clubs where people meet, socialize, and share tips with each other. Many are open to doing deals with other investors. Just put "real estate investment clubs" and your city into any search engine and up will come many results that match your query.

Where I live in Arizona there are many different real estate investment groups, some by city level, others by county or state level. The entry fees are nominal and you get out of them what you put in. If you are a novice, you need to be in one of these groups.

Each state has some different rules about foreclosures and how they are processed. A local real estate investment group will let you know what the rules and customs are where you live.

I also want to talk about risk. If you're looking for an investment strategy where there is no risk, put your money in a bank savings account. They currently pay half of one percent interest! Of course there are risks in investing in real estate. This book is intended to give you the knowledge to *minimize* those risks so that the odds act greatly in your favor.

Of the 200 or so properties that I purchased at auction myself over the past 12 years, there were a few...very

few...that I did not make money on. Certain things like extensive repairs that were not visible upon inspection and therefore not planned for happened. Sometimes the insurance that I got the minute I acquired the property paid for the repairs, sometimes not. I have also made $50k or more on a single transaction! In the aggregate, my investment strategies and experience have made me a lot of money. I live a lifestyle that many would envy. I drive what I want, I live in a lovely home, and I live a self-directed life.

Slow and steady like the turtle has always been my formula to extraordinary profits in the space of buying houses at auction. I have seen countless hundreds of amateurs (rabbits) enter this space and exit just as quickly. Slow and steady wins the race every time.

Rick Rickert

That's really the end result I want all my readers to have. A self-directed life. When you realize how few people ever get to do that you will realize what a gift and blessing that is!

Yes, investing in real estate, especially through the foreclosure auction is fun and exciting, but the real reward at the end of the day is the freedom you will have to do what you want, when you want. That's priceless!

So take this book, and draw up a plan to buy your first investment property at the auction. Set deadlines for yourself when you will have certain activities completed. Be accountable to yourself to get them done.

My best advice to new real estate investors is trust what you know, be bold, and jump in. Buying at public auction is great because while being bold, you can jump in right away. Bid today, pay tomorrow, and you're in your project the following day. If you're a beginner, stay in areas that are close to home and that you know well.

Align yourself with a real estate agent that understands what an investor needs. Starting out, I made the mistake of using a friend in real estate instead of an agent that knew how to handle my needs as an investor. We clashed on everything! As an investor, I knew the value of listing during the remodel process and it worked well for me as about 40% of my listings went under contract during the remodel process. It's all about the turn and maximizing the profit. It was out of this

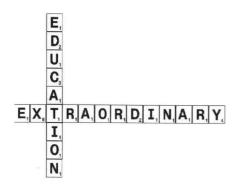

frustration that I got my real estate license back in 1999 for the purpose of saving a few bucks and having hassle-free listings. My point is, friends and family are not always the best team members when investing in real estate. I never list properties other than my own. When investing, it's important for me to keep my focus on the task at hand. If I take on other people's listings typically something is going to suffer. Don't let your deals suffer ever! Sometimes you have to make tough decisions, but investing your own dollars into real estate is serious and needs your full attention.

I know many people who over educate themselves and never buy a single piece of real estate. That's a shame! Your best education is going to come from doing your first deal, and the confidence boost you will get out of it will be unforgettable. I've made mistakes while investing, but every one of them made me a better investor. Never investing at all would have been an even greater mistake. Please think twice before you pay some guru tens of thousands of dollars for their coaching package. Your best education will come from doing! Remember, you need to factor the cost of your education and coaching (including the cost of this book) into your next deal or deals over the next year. I'm sure I just shocked many readers as they are recalculating their deals. Education is a cost of doing business.

If you're a Realtor, know that 50% of all real estate transactions nationwide involve investors. Agents, brokers, and brokerages are suffering as they are trying to reinvent themselves with respect to traditional real estate, yet do nothing to serve the real estate investor community. Let me point to the obvious. Traditional home buyers will buy a home from you every three to five years and then only if you stay in touch with them on a monthly basis with your marketing collateral so they don't forget about you. Real estate investors are always on the hunt for great deals and have the ability to buy from you multiple times per year. Most agents I run into are not serving investors because they haven't stepped out of the "MLS shell" and looked to offer them something new and valuable like the new supply of inventory available at public auction! Reinvent what you are offering. I've built a successful business around this.

If after reading this book you're still stumped, call me at 480-686-9945.

Important Concepts

1. Commit to mastering this subject.
2. Create what legacy looks like for you.
3. Create what your life style will be and start living it.

Special Bonus

I am so committed to seeing you get going and succeed, I will give anyone reading this book a free 30 minute consultation with me or one of my experienced staff, by calling 480-686-9945. All of my staff are licensed real estate agents in the State of Arizona and have at least 5 years bidding experience at the auction. They can answer any question or if it's state specific, can point you in the right direction to get the information you want. When you call, we will set up a phone appointment. If you're in Arizona or nearby, you can visit our office complex inside the Bank of America building in Mesa, AZ. It's your choice.

Appendix 1

Max Bid Sheet

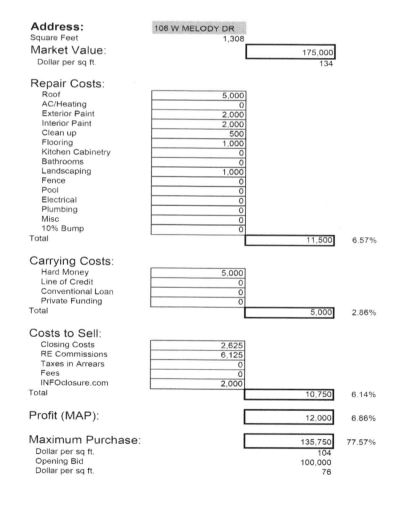

Address: 106 W MELODY DR

Square Feet	1,308

Market Value: 175,000
Dollar per sq ft. 134

Repair Costs:

Roof	5,000	
AC/Heating	0	
Exterior Paint	2,000	
Interior Paint	2,000	
Clean up	500	
Flooring	1,000	
Kitchen Cabinetry	0	
Bathrooms	0	
Landscaping	1,000	
Fence	0	
Pool	0	
Electrical	0	
Plumbing	0	
Misc	0	
10% Bump	0	
Total	11,500	6.57%

Carrying Costs:

Hard Money	5,000	
Line of Credit	0	
Conventional Loan	0	
Private Funding	0	
Total	5,000	2.86%

Costs to Sell:

Closing Costs	2,625	
RE Commissions	6,125	
Taxes in Arrears	0	
Fees	0	
INFOclosure.com	2,000	
Total	10,750	6.14%

Profit (MAP): 12,000 6.86%

Maximum Purchase: 135,750 77.57%

Dollar per sq ft.	104
Opening Bid	100,000
Dollar per sq ft.	76

Closing Remarks

It has been my pleasure to be your host for the preceding 12 chapters. It is my hope that you will utilize the information to create something more than just income for yourself. I feel so fortunate to have been able to create income streams through a variety of ways all focused around buying at auction.

Starting in 1998, I bought my first property and made income from the profit. Over time I started to bid for other investors and collected a flat fee for that service. On occasion, those same investors requested that I list the home for them, thus creating another income stream. One stream I turned down was income from doing property management. I choose not to manage properties and thus leave that income stream to someone who will perform a better service than me. I have made income from wholesaling properties. One of the most interesting income streams is collecting a fee for assisting a home owner in retrieving their equity though the excess proceeds process. I am earning income for selling franchises and private label opportunities to other professionals seeking to service investors entering this space of public auction. Lastly, I have earned income from teaching the subject of buying at public auction. I think that's about eight streams of income.

Having money in hand is important, but one of the most rewarding things about being in this space is the ability to educate people on buying at auction. It is great to see the faces of people when they connect with the concept and are truly excited to buy in this space.

We all have to do something in life to generate income and feed our families. Fortunately I was able to find something that I have been able to create great income from and also remain very passionate about. Buying at auction has served me well since 1998. What I started out doing then has evolved into something exciting and profitable. Don't wait to jump in. If you are ready, make it happen. Now is that time and trust that what it looks like today going in may not be what is looks like in 3, 5 or 10 years.

If this subject is of interest to you but you are still struggling with getting started feel free to contact us at the following email address: info@infoclosure.com. We would love to help you get started.